Ascent of the Simple Soul to the Sublime State of Divine Union

Ascent of the Simple Soul to the Sublime State of Divine Union

Philip Francis Healey, o.c.d.s.

Belleville, Ontario, Canada

Ascent of the Simple Soul to the Sublime State of Divine Union

Copyright © 2002, Philip F. Healy

All Scripture quotations, unless otherwise specified, are taken from *The New American Bible* copyright © 1970 and 1986 Confraternity of Christian Doctrine, Washington, D.C.

Scripture quotations marked JB are taken from *The Jerusalem Bible*, copyright © 1966, 1967 and 1968 by Darton, Longman & Todd Ltd. and Doubleday & Company, Inc.

Scripture quotations marked NASB are taken from the *New American Standard Bible*, copyright © The Lockman Foundation 1960, 1962, 1963, 1968, 1971, 1972, 1973. All rights reserved.

Scripture quotations marked NJB are taken from *The New Jerusalem Bible* copyright © 1985 by Darton, Longman & Todd Ltd. and Doubleday.

Cover art by Kathleen Healy Bianco, incorporating part of Michelangelo's creation scene on the celing of the Sistene Chapel in the Vatican.

Gaelic translation courtesy of Daithí Ó Loideáin, B.A.

ISBN: 1-55306-362-7

For more information, please contact:

Philip F. Healy
145 Laauwe Avenue, Wayne, New Jersey 07470 USA

Essence Publishing is a Christian Book Publisher dedicated to furthering the work of Christ through the written word. *Guardian Books* is an imprint of *Essence Publishing*.

Dedication

This book is dedicated to my wife,
Hannah Catherine,
upon whose suggestion it was undertaken;
and
also to each of our children,
their spouses,
and
our grandchildren.

Author

PHILIP FRANCIS HEALY, M. DIV., D. Min., O.C.D.S., is a Third Order Discalced Carmelite who has been involved in pastoral ministry since 1981, and in spiritual guidance since 1985. He has spent his adult life in the study of spiritual theology, including mysticism and contemplative prayer, in addition to formal seminary studies in theology, Scripture, and pastoral ministry. Prior to his retirement in 1993, he worked as a professional engineer as a graduate of City University of New York in 1955.

Born in Manhattan in 1928 of Irish immigrant parents, Maurice and Johanna, he attended parochial schools in the Bronx and Queens before the family moved to Ireland. There he attended Ardfert National School and the Christian Brothers' Secondary School in The Green, Tralee, County Kerry. Returning to the U.S.A. in 1943, he finished high school and entered C.U.N.Y. in 1947. During 1950 to 1952, he served in an engineering construction battalion in the U.S. Army, attaining the rank of sergeant first-class.

He and his wife, Hannah, have six children and several grandchildren. All of their children have worked their way through college taking graduate degrees in Law, Business, Education, Science, Exercise Physiology, and Nutrition.

Acknowledgements

T HIS BOOK IS THE RESULT OF A lifetime of study and reflection on spiritual theology, mysticism, and contemplation. I am indebted to my mentors *ex libris:* Thomas Merton, John of the Cross, and Teresa of Avila read in my earlier years; and all those authors subsequently read in my *lectio divina.* My indebtedness also extends to all those authors on the *New Mysticism* of the thirteenth and fourteenth centuries, including the Rhineland mystics; especially, Marguerite Porete and our modern authors revisiting and reviving this aspect of spirituality.

Especially, I thankfully wish to acknowledge Rosalie Scudellari, B.A. in Math., M.A. in Theology, for her encouragement to write this book after many previous discussions and dialogues on the subject. Without this encouragement and my wife's suggestion to write, this book might not have been written. Ms. Scudellari has made the production of this book possible by her many hours of typing, proofing, reviewing, and revisions.

I also thank my family for their support and patience in regard to this effort; especially, my daughter Kathleen and my son James.

Table of Contents

Preface

I N THE LAST FEW YEARS, THIS AUTHOR has been confronted with a new investigation into the little-known ontological state of loss of self or "No-self," following the overpassing of the soul to the sublimest state of divine union attainable in this life. This investigation has been inspired by spiritual and literary writers revisiting the *New Mysticism* of the High Middle Ages, some who have currently experienced "No-self" or the "falling away of self," and others who have been interfaced with spiritual Web sites and forums on the Internet and have taken on the search.

The "No-self" is the result of the falling away of the "I—Thou" relationship with the Divine, wherein the will (of the soul having totally and irrevocably abandoned itself to God) is annihilated so that only God's will is willing in the soul. Here the soul finds itself in a state of nothingness. This presents it with the problem of the awareness of its reality, and how to live in and cope with this new life of "being" in God. This need is what gives the impetus to the writing of this book. It is written, hopefully, to help those who have reached this unfamiliar state, or are approaching it, albeit vaguely cognizant of its significance, so that they may find solace and assurance in regard to the soul's new state of being. Further to this, the book serves to acquaint those who would seek perfection with the nature of the most sublime divine union that is possible to reach in this life; a union tasting of glory to which we are all called and for which we can strive assiduously and avidly.

This undertaking attempts also to include and integrate into one spiritual treatise a major proportion of the corpus of ideas and information available (although scant) relevant to its subject.

Solemn Commemoration of Our Lady of Mount Carmel
July 16th, 2001 — In honor of the Mystical Rose

PHILIP FRANCIS HEALY, O.C.D.S.

$\mathcal{F}$oreword

THIS BOOK IS ABOUT THE DIVINE, the One Who Is, Who pursues us with a love of such vehemence that it is beyond all telling; a God Who invites us to be one with Him for all eternity. The book is written, hopefully, for His greater glory and honor, that it may be beneficial and encouraging to souls seeking meaning in life. It is offered in a pastoral sense to assist in opening the way for such souls to seek the Lord through spiritual development.

John (1 Jn 4:16) tells us, *"God is love, and he who abides in love abides in God, and God in him."* This tells us that we can have being in God, and that He allows us to be the abode of His Being if we have His love within. There is no doubt that there is a universal call to this union with God when we read Scripture; particularly John, chapters 14 and 17. We also have assurance of this call in the Church's pronouncements in chapters two and five of *Lumen gentium* of Vatican II (Abbott, SJ, 1966: pp 15-18). Peter (1 Pt 2:9) calls all those of faith in God, *"a royal priesthood, a holy people set apart,"* because they are united to the body of Christ. Sharing in the royal priesthood means that we can offer ourselves as an oblation to God through our sacrifices in our pilgrimage here on earth. This calls for us to despoil ourselves of all that is not of God, by allowing His grace to work within us. This universal call is an invitation to reach, by His grace, the most sublime state of divine union possible in this life known as "union without distinction" (*unitas indistinctionis*), which is the subject of this book.

This work, intended as religious and scholarly research, has attempted to give insight into this closest union with the Divine attainable in this life, and to describe its possibilities of being reached by His grace, providing we dispose ourselves and work to receive such an unspeakable gift. It is a challenge requiring fortitude, perseverance, humility, and generosity. The insight offered is given in the context of the overpassing of the soul from the traditionally-known union of distinction or *unio mystica* to union of indistinction.

The plan of this book is to give a didactic treatise on the spiritual journey of the soul in its pursuit of the Divine through the perfection of love, walking the way of the Cross (*via Crucis*) in spiritual combat. It is presented as a mystical itinerary in Part I. In Part II, some ways, means, aids, and practices for advancement to divine union are given. It is further noted here, that the way to this union is along the path of love (*cursus amoris*), humility, and complete surrender. The emphasis is on love in this journey, even over knowledge: "It can be said that God is sought less through intellectual considerations than by the heart's pressing need (Cf. Thomas Philippe, O.P. in *Angelicum,* Vol. 14, 1937)." (Goichon, 1959: p.28).

This treatise is written in the context of the present

reawakening of the *New Mysticism* of the thirteenth and fourteenth centuries now being experienced, and about which increasingly more currently is being written (see "Bibliography"). It seeks to emphasize that the approach to this sublime union of indistinction, a union of being called *wesenmystik,* is open to all the faithful to taste and see (*gustate et videte*) the goodness of the Lord—a taste even of eternal life—in an awesome sense of a tremendous mystery (*mysterium tremendum*). References and quotations from this research are employed, as required, to lend authenticity to the treatise, with additional commentaries by the author, to reveal the sense or the ineffability of the *New Mysticism* experiences presented. They also illustrate the corpus of scholarly work existent (albeit scarce and in great dearth) regarding aspects of this *New Mysticism,* much of which has been integrated into this one volume as a spiritual treatise not found by the author to be heretofore readily available.

Sources for this book are the mystical and spiritual works of well-recognized authors on the subject of spiritual theology. Writers to whom reference is made from the period of *New Mysticism* are: Beatrijs of Nazareth, Mechthild of Magdeburg, Hadewijch of Brabant, Jacopone da Todi, Marguerite Porete of Hainault; and somewhat later, Meister Eckhart, a Dominican friar. Thomas Aquinas, a contemporary of St. Francis, was used as a source in this period, although not of the *New Mysticism* effort per se. Sixteenth-century sources include: John of the Cross (the mystical doctor) and Teresa of Avila (the doctor of prayer). Ending the nineteenth century and thereafter, sources are: Thérèse of Lisieux, Elizabeth of the Trinity, and Gabriel of St. Mary Magdalen, all Carmelites. The more contemporary ones used are: Jordan Aumann, Thomas Dubay, Amélie Goichon, Amy Hollywood, Bernard McGinn, Emilie Zum Brunn, and Georgette Epiney-Burgard.

Extreme caution must be applied to the reading of mystical writings, especially for the uninitiated in the spiritual life and even the proficient. This caveat applies to the works of John of the Cross, Teresa of Avila, and the Rhineland mystics—Hadewijch, Marguerite Porete, and Meister Eckhart, especially. The particular problem in the reading of these writings are:

A. Mystical language is by nature quite ambiguous and, if taken *prima facie* (on the face of it) or literally, it can be grossly misinterpreted. Mystical experiences are extremely difficult to articulate because they come from God.

B. For those who avidly seek inordinate supernatural experiences or spiritually sensational phenomena, mystical writings may lead such astray. This is because the union sought in the mystical way is not a matter of the phenomena accidental to attaining it, but that which progresses interiorly, almost imperceptibly.

C. There is the danger for beginners and those not yet very proficient in the spiritual life, that they may imagine that the experiences of which they read are happening to themselves and are misled thereby.

D. Those in the early stages of the way of perfection

may be prone to follow the way indicated by their mystical reading, while forsaking the spiritual path through which they are being lead by the Lord as being most appropriate for them.

Marguerite Porete in her book *The Mirror* (Crawford, 1981: pp.19-20) recognized the difficulty attached to understanding her book. She was so concerned with this and the chance that some person(s) of authority in the Church might misunderstand it, that she sought the approval of three men of learning and holiness. These were: a Franciscan friar, a Cistercian monk, and a theologian. None could find fault with the book. However, the first of them said that if it is to be understood, this will be due to the working of the Holy Spirit, and not to the reader's learning. This meant that its inspiration was not for everyone, and he said that whoever is incapable of its understanding should have the book kept from him. The second person found it to be in full accordance with the Scriptures, as well as all that was written to be true. The last to give approval added a warning that many should not see it lest they abandon the life to which they were called, and embrace one to which they will never arrive.

Its words cut deep, and can only be appreciated by the few who have advanced beyond the early stages of the way of perfection. They can only come there through God's action, not their own: this is the way God works (Crawford, 1981: p.20).

Those who would read such works as *The Mirror,* or others of those given above, and even this book, should patiently and humbly follow the path or way to which they are called, and await God's action to bring them to perfect union should He deem it timely and efficacious for them. The Lord works in His own time to accomplish His works in us, all to our benefit.

Porete (Babinsky, 1993: p.79) expresses the difficulty in poetic form:

> *You who would read this book,*
> *If you indeed wish to grasp it,*
> *Think about what you say,*
> *For it is very difficult to comprehend;*
> *Humility, who is keeper of the treasury*
> *of Knowledge*
> *And the mother of the other Virtues,*
> *Must overtake you.*
>
> *Theologians and other clerks,*
> *You will not have the intellect for it,*
> *No matter how brilliant your abilities,*
> *If you do not proceed humbly.*
> *And may Love and Faith, together,*
> *Cause you to rise above Reason,*
> *[Since] they are the ladies of the house.*
>
> *Even Reason witnesses*
> *In the Thirteenth Chapter of this book,*
> *And with no shame about it,*
> *That Love and Faith make her live*
> *And she does not free herself from them,*
> *For they have lordship over her,*
> *Which is why she must humble herself.*
>
> *Humble, then, your wisdom*
> *Which is based on Reason,*

And place all your fidelity
In those things which are given
By Love, illuminated through Faith.
And thus you will understand this book
Which makes the Soul live by love.

It is my sincere prayer that those who read this book will not be misled or misguided by lack of its understanding; that our divine Lord will guide them to understand it sufficiently to receive it and derive from it the meaning intended to assist them in reaching the fruition of their spiritual journey to the Triune God. May God be adored, honored, praised, and glorified forever.

Ar son glóir agus onóir Dé
For the glory and honor of God

GUSTATE ET VIDETE

Introduction

THIS BOOK IS NOT WRITTEN FOR the faint-hearted. It is a challenge for those courageous souls who have decided to commit themselves to God in a life of love. Hopefully in its exposition it will serve to encourage souls to embark on such a life, and to point the way, at least, in some general fashion.

To accomplish this, the book is divided into two parts. Part I is an exposition of the spiritual journey which embraces a certain commonality with the multitude of variations unique to individual spiritual itineraries. It is recognized that all who follow the way to union with God travel the same path, albeit with uniquely differing experiences and consciousness. "The spiritual life is a dynamic and interior mystery that accommodates itself to the personality and existential situation of the individual" (Aumann, 1980: p.20). Part II deals with the means and practices for advancement in holiness and toward disposing oneself for union with the Divine.

We intend to speak of Christian spirituality in this volume, and more particularly that spirituality found in the Catholic tradition. We define "Christian spirituality" simply as the lived encounter with Jesus Christ in the Spirit bringing us to the Father.

Similarly, Vatican Council II in *Gaudium et Spes,* n.22 (Abbott, SJ, 1966: pp.220-222)...

> affirms that there is only one spirituality for all, and it consists in a participation in the mystery of Christ. Christian spirituality is therefore a participation in the mystery of Christ through the interior life of grace, actuated by faith, charity, and the other Christian virtues... it is ... the life of God in the august mystery of the Trinity (Aumann, 1980: pp. 17,18).

The love of God, actualized in our lives to its greatest possibilities here and now, is the essence of Christian perfection. It is not any specific sort of spiritual exercise or practice that produces saints, but simply the attainment of the perfect love of God.

Pope Pius XII, in his frequent pronouncements, seems to emphasize that a profoundly spiritual Catholic laity is of great need in the Church.

In whatever calling or state in life, be it clerical or lay, religious or secular, all Christians who strive for sanctity must utilize the general means of sanctification. The Catholic laity (as with clergy and religious) are advised to cultivate the theological virtues (faith, hope, and charity) and moral virtues, to be faithful to the practice of prayer, to mortify themselves in light of seeking perfect detachment from all created things, even spiritual gifts or consolations, and, through the liturgy, to seek union with Christ. However, such a soul must make use of all these means in conformity with the duties of one's state in life.

Above all, the soul in this world seeking perfection will strive to do God's will in everything great or small so as to arrive at total "abandonment to the will of God"; even to the annihilation of its own will. This is the "royal road to transformation in Christ" (Goichon, 1959: Jkt. Rev.).

But this soul may ask, "How is it possible to live the spiritual life of silent and profound union with God in our world, in which practically all the requisite conditions for it seem to be non-existent—a world of disorder and an apparent disunity between the soul's interior and exterior life?" Nevertheless, many souls have, and are, living this profound spiritual life notwithstanding the disorder of the world and apparent disunity of soul because, although they are part of the world, they have learned to live as to be not of it. They can flourish, for essentially the spiritual life

…is an unfolding, a flowering of the baptismal grace which every Christian receives, and the fullest development of the graces of all the other sacraments (Goichon, 1959: p.x).

Sublime perfection in this life seeks to exclude anything which "impedes the totality of the affective movement toward God" (Aumann, 1980: p.117).

Different patterns of Christian living appeal to certain groups or individuals suited to their personality, temperament, charisms, and calling in life. Sometimes it finds its expression as a so-called school of spirituality in a corporate way or personal following, as: Benedictine,

Franciscan, Dominican, Carmelite, Salesian, Teresian, San Juanist, Cistercian, Carthusian, or Victorine. It may find a uniqueness in groups such as the Third Orders, the beguines, and beghards; or, be classified by culture (French or Spanish); or, by a doctrinal/devotional basis (Eucharistic spirituality and Marian spirituality).

> The schools of spirituality are thus an indication of the diversity of the ways of the Spirit, a proof of the Church's respect for personal freedom in following the impulses of the Spirit, and a corporate witness to the variety of ways in which the mystery of Christ is imaged in the Mystical Body of the Church (Aumann, 1980: pp.33,34).

Further on, we will dwell upon the spirituality of the *New Mysticism* of the Middle Ages, particularly that of the Rhineland mystics, the beguines, Meister Eckhart, medieval holy women such as Hildegard, Mechthild, Beatrijs, Hadewijch, and Porete; and also, that of Jacopone and the "Victorines."

Part One

SPIRITUAL ITINERARY

CHAPTER ONE

The Soul's Pursuit

I N THIS LIFE, OUR SOUL IS IN PURSUIT of joy, even if it does not understand what true joy is or where to seek to find it. Some seek it in pleasure, power, and riches; others may seek it in family, art, music, and spirituality.

The pursuit is the impetus for some to embrace the self-reliant behavior touted by modern popular psychologists and business management educators, which centers them in their own powers of self, rather than in God. In this psychologism, the emphasis is on self-fulfillment through the individual's own ability for self-actualization, self-development, self-esteem, and self-control. Susan Muto (1991: p.12) sees this as "a self-alone" myth which self-destructs:

> Psychologism is incredibly 'self-,' not God-, centered. It is rooted in the basic illusion of 'hubris,' in the deceptive, pride-filled mentality that I or 'we' alone can mold, manage, and maintain our "act" without reference to a Higher Power. The

self-alone myth is based on so false a premise that it inevitably self-destructs.

When the pursuit ends in self-fulfillment in reaching goals defined by humanism and culture, there is no true joy; the soul is not satisfied in its spirit and seeks something beyond its state of ego-desperation.

Should some seek joy in other human endeavors or gifts, in family, art, music and even things of heaven short of the Divine, they will not be sated in spirit. This is because the soul seeks true and lasting joy which can be attained only through consummate and sublime union with God for Whom it only has affinity and to Whom it must return for satiety.

The vicissitudes of life coupled with our search for joy may bring us to a spiritual awakening, to an affective contact with the living God our Creator. Certain graces begin to flow from the Lord into such souls evoking responses to His promptings and drawing them ever closer to Him as Pursuer. These souls turn inward to find Him and may experience His consolations, delights, wounds of love, feelings, and even spiritual touches which taste of eternal life. Even these joys leave the soul unsated because they are given to entice and draw the soul to deeper union with God. The joys are not the end, but the means along the road to a more profound union. Therefore, they must not be clung to in reaching for the sublimest of all pursuits.

The mystical doctor St. John of the Cross, reminiscent of Mary of Bethany, sister of Martha, writes that we are all called to the summit of union and to regard it as the sole necessary pursuit, as Fr. Thomas Dubay (1989: p.211) so beautifully expresses it:

Thomas Merton (1977: pp.340,341) expressed this in his poem:

> *If you seek a heavenly light*
> *I, solitude, am your professor.*
>
> *For, I, Solitude, am thine own self;*
> *I, Nothingness, am thy all.*
> *I, Silence, thy Amen!*

Solitude is being alone with the Lord, being aware of His presence even amidst the noise and activity of the world, and opening ourselves in silence to receive His secret (mystical) encounters. So we must endeavor to provide and allow for conditions which favor solitude.

We are all capable of receiving mystical experiences. We do so when we embrace our humanity, one which finds its fulfillment in living in the awareness of God's presence.

The modern theologian Karl Rahner writes of devout Christians: "...the devout Christian of the future will either be a "mystic," one who has "experienced" something, or he will cease to be anything at all" (Rahner, 1971: p.15). Divine presence is the basic category for speaking of the mystical experience of God. Teresa of Avila writes of this presence:

> This presence is a great favor from God and should be highly esteemed by the one He gives it to, for it is a very sublime prayer, but is not a vision; in this prayer of union or quiet one understands that God is present by the effects that, as I say, He grants to the soul—that is the way His Majesty wants to give the experience of Himself (Cunningham, et al, 1996: p.124).

Mysticism is a "radical, transforming love of God," while the "mystic is one whose single-minded love of God and love of neighbor leads to an awareness of the presence of God" (Cunningham, et al, 1996: p.128).

CHAPTER TWO

Spiritual Perfection— Christian Spirituality

WHEN SPEAKING OF THE COMMAND to love, Jesus tells us, *"You must be made perfect as your heavenly Father is perfect"* (Mt 5:48). This raises the question of what constitutes perfection and how is it possible to be made perfect as our Father in heaven.

St. Teresa of Avila, when addressing her fellow nuns, answered the first part of the question for us:

> Be sure, my daughters, that true perfection consists in the love of God and our neighbour, and the better we keep both these commandments the more perfect we shall be (St. Teresa, 1930: p.22).

This is based on Scripture:

> *The love of God consists in this: that we keep His commandments—and His commandments are not burdensome* (1 Jn 5:3).

No one has ever seen God. Yet if we love one
another God dwells in us, and His love is brought
to perfection in us (1 Jn 4:12).

When we possess the love of God, we reflect His
love back to Him in requital and extend it in charity in
love of neighbor. We see this also in Scripture: *"Love,*
then, consists in this: not that we have loved God but
that He has loved us" (1 Jn 4:10), and *"We, for our part,*
love because He first loved us" (1 Jn 4:19). When this
love is brought to perfection in us, it reflects the perfection of the Father because we love with His love.
This view may help to understand a possible resolu-
tion to the dilemma of the second part of the question
posed above, especially in light of the teaching of John
of the Cross, "that a soul can love God as much as it is
loved by Him [cf. "Spiritual Canticle, Stanza 37" (Goichon, 1959: p.169, n.32)].

We do not find St. Thomas Aquinas speak of the
contemplative mode of life in his treatise *De Perfec-*
tione Vitae Spiritualis, notwithstanding his familiari-
ty with it. He evaluated perfection according to the
degree of perfection of charity attained, not the mode
of life, in view of St. Paul's First Epistle to the
Corinthians (1 Cor 13). To express it differently, St.
Thomas measured the level of perfection reached in
terms of the love of God surpassing that of temporal
goods and the use of one's own free will. Another measure of it, he used, was the perfection of our love of
neighbor. In 1 John 4:20 we see that love of our ene-
mies is "presented to us as a means of imitating the
perfection of our Father in heaven" (Goichon, 1959:
pp.30,31). Goichon (1959: p.180, n.49; p.48) notes,

But for St. Thomas Aquinas, the summit of wisdom and of human perfection is to love with a real love the supremely personal principle of all that exists, that is to say, in response to His love which first loved us, and... which descends within us and overflows from us to make us continue His work in time and communicate His goodness.

Perfection is attained when there is nothing left in the soul that prevents its affection from being totally oriented toward God, then the soul loves God as much as it is loved by Him, since it leaves unused none of the grace that God pours into it. This is precisely the meaning of the spirit of childhood, which flies to God with a fullness of love devoid of reservations and selfish motives. It also implies a constant docility to the gifts of the Holy Ghost. That is why the deep purifications of St. Thérèse of Lisieux [usually associated with the contemplative life] were accomplished with so much calm and without the painful repercussions of the "night of the soul" so common among the saints of earlier centuries.

Being a contemplative is not required for salvation. A contemplative life is a gratuitous gift of God to those souls disposed to it. However, one must not be distressed should another way to union be one's calling, although it may demand more faith, perseverance, and tougher labor. More merit may be gained as a consequence of humbling oneself to resignation of such a way. We can aspire to contemplation by disposing ourselves through the practice of seeking perfection in our spiritual life, and being pleased to take the lowest place as our Lord taught by word and deed (Lk 14:10). St. Teresa (Kavanaugh, 1980: p.99) instructed her charges,

> So not because all in this house practice prayer must all be contemplatives; that's impossible. And it would be very distressing for the one who isn't a contemplative if she didn't understand the truth that to be a contemplative is a gift from God; and since being one isn't necessary for salvation, nor does God demand this, she shouldn't think anyone will demand it of her. So, you will not fail to be very perfect if you do what has been mentioned. Indeed, it could be that a Sister will gain much more merit because she must work harder and the Lord leads her as one who is strong, [like Martha] saving for her what she doesn't enjoy here below so as to give it to her all at once. Not for this reason should she grow fainthearted or give up prayer... for sometimes the Lord comes very late and pays just as well, and all at once, what He was giving to others in the course of many years.

St. Teresa, mentions the practice of three important things which we should follow in seeking perfection: (1) love for one another; (2) detachment from all created things; and, (3) true humility (Kavanaugh, 1980: p.54). To this we would like to add, which is presumptive in her instruction, to pray always (Lk 18:1). The humility referred to is that evoked by the image of a little child:

> *Unless you turn and become like children, you will not enter the kingdom of heaven* [nor that kingdom even attained in this life]. *Whoever*

humbles himself like this child is the greatest in the kingdom of heaven (Mt 18:3-4; Gospel for the feast of St. Thérèse of the Child Jesus).

The *Little Way* and the trial of faith of St. Thérèse (Little Flower) are compatible with every state of life.

Elizabeth of the Trinity, when asked about her idea of holiness, gave the reply, "To live by love." When asked further how quickest to attain it, she replied, "To become very little, to surrender oneself irrevocably." She offers us a thought on her posthumous mission:

I think that in heaven my mission will be to draw souls by helping them to go out of themselves in order to cling to God by a wholly simple and loving movement and to keep them in this great silence within which will allow God to communicate Himself to them and to transform them into Himself (Kane, 1984: pp.28,29).

She extols the riches of every Christian, which she says is situated in the most fundamental level of lay spirituality:

While affirming her happiness in her Carmelite vocation, the mystic goes beyond external forms to enlarge on the common riches of every Christian, whether in the monastery or in the midst of the world with its multiple activities: God's desire to give Himself to us, our baptism, the Eucharist, our destiny beyond death, the universal presence of God, the reality of the "Three" in us, the joy of being a beloved child of the God of Love, a joy which impels us to give ourselves to others. In this way her message assumes universal meaning (Kane, 1984: p.27).

It is especially noted that in her trinitarian approach to spirituality, Elizabeth of the Trinity remains Christocentric and that,

> Whether in the cloister or in the world, Elizabeth recognizes only one Christian way, that of love in everything, and of attention to God present and pervenient (Kane, 1984: pp.87,88).

The surest way of perfection and availing ourselves of salvation is to imitate Christ and to keep the commandments, a way beautifully presented by Thomas à Kempis in his *Imitation of Christ*. Jesus says, *"There is One who is good. If you wish to enter into life, keep the commandments"* (Mt 19:17). *"Whoever wishes to come after me, must deny himself, take up his cross, and follow me"* (Mt 16:24).

Whoever would seek union with God must take up his or her cross and seek to do only the will of God. One

> must be willing to be tossed to and fro under the action of God's [permissive] will, and to see his "works" crumble to nothing if it so please God. Whatever happens, he says: "In manus tuus commendo spiritum meum," [Into Your hands I commend my spirit]... He becomes a window through which Christ looks down upon the world, and a mirror in which the world sees itself in the Heart of Christ (Goichon, 1959: p.xiii).

We should also add, *"Whether, then, you eat or drink or whatever you do, do all to the glory of God"* (1 Cor

10:31; NASB). Then the soul can joyfully sing, "I have found Him whom my soul loveth; and I will not let Him go…" [Cant. 3:4; from the Epistle for the Feast of St. Mary Magdalen (Goichon, 1959: p.xiv)].

We must, therefore, not delude ourselves into thinking that there is an easy way to union with God. The road is hard, fraught with the wiles and temptations of the devil, the concupiscence of the flesh, and the allurements of the world. We must suffer as Christ did and, thereby, share in His sufferings which He has left for us to undergo. The more we are purified to reach greater perfection, the more keen the pain of suffering. It is as if we were being refined in a crucible, a spoliation and an immolation when reaching the summit of union.

The senses and the faculties (will, intellect, memory, and imagination) are ordered to the Divine. Although salvation is availed of and attained by the soul through basic obeisance to the commandments, the royal road of perfection is of untold merit and wins a higher place in the heavenly mansion; our meriting being vicarious through Christ, Who only can merit condignly.

"If the soul has undergone a transformation in Christ as total as He wished," then it may enter beatitude without passing through purgatory:

> If charity is purified in purgatory, it is done without the gaining of merit, since merit belongs to the wayfaring state; if, on the other hand, the degree of charity of the glorified soul corresponds to the degree to which it is loved by the One who has predestined it, we must conclude that a soul that enters beatitude without passing through purgatory, without needing purification,

has loved God here on earth (even if only at the instant of death) as much as it was loved by Him. In other words, such a soul was, if even for that one instant, perfectly faithful to the grace received [Maritain, "The Degrees of Knowledge," appendix 8 (Goichon, 1959: p.169, n. 32)].

When we suffer the revilement of our fellow men and women patiently, we earn glory in heaven:

Blest are you when they insult you and persecute you and utter every kind of slander against you because of me. Be glad and rejoice for your reward is great in heaven; they persecuted the prophets before you in the very same way (Mt 5:11,12).

St. Paul also puts our sufferings into perspective:

The present burden of our trial is light enough, and earns for us an eternal weight of glory beyond all comparison (2 Cor 4:17).

Traditionally, some mountains or "high places" have been revered as sacred places in biblical times. We find references to this in both the Hebrew and New Testament accounts. We read of Mount Sinai where Moses encountered *Yahweh* (I Am Who Am) and received the tablets of the Decalogue during the Exodus. The Samarians worshiped God on Mount Gerizim. Mount Moriah, the place of Abraham's intended sacrifice of Isaac, became the site of Solomon's Temple; now, the site of the Islamic Dome of the Rock. Our Lord's transfiguration took place on Mount Tabor, and He gave us the Beatitudes on the Mount of Beatitudes. Elijah came to Mount

Horeb (Sinai) and, there, at the entrance of a cave, encountered the Lord of Hosts in a tiny whispering sound. He had earlier lived in a cave on Mount Carmel facing the sea, not far from the *place of sacrifice* (El-Muhraqa), known as the Wadi-ain-es-siah where the Order of the Brothers of the Blessed Virgin Mary of Mount Carmel built the first Carmelite monastery in the early thirteenth century. Jesus suffered His passion in Gethsemane in the Mount of Olives.

Christian spiritual writers have adopted the image of the climbing of a mountain (stairs or ladder) as analogous to an ascent to God in our journey to Union. The ascent entails steps or stages toward advancement as utilized by St. John Climachus in *Ladder of Divine Ascent* on his thirty steps toward perfection. St. Bernard of Clairvaux writes of four stages of love in his treatise, *On the Love of God,* by which we: (1) Love ourselves for the sake of ourselves; (2) love God for the sake of His gifts; (3) love God for His Own sake only; and finally, (4) love ourselves only for the sake of God. St. John of the Cross uses the ascent of Mt. Carmel in presenting his three stages: (1) beginners; (2) proficients; and, (3) the perfect— punctuated by his two *dark nights*. We will treat more fully with this subject later.

Donald Gallagher, Ph.D. (1991: p.60) reiterates St. John of the Cross' brief little poem on the "Sum of Perfection":

> *Forgetfulness of creatures*
> *Mindfulness of the Creator*
> *Attentiveness to the Interior Self*
> *Responsiveness to the Beloved in loving*

Forgetfulness...

Turning away more and more from the created things of this world.

Mindfulness...

Turning ever more toward the Infinite Creator.

Attentiveness...

Delving ever more deeply into the Interior of Oneself. In search not of one's individuality, but of the Divine Spark.

Responsiveness...

In loving response, answering Love's call, replying to the Beloved.

CHAPTER THREE

The Pilgrim's Itinerary

T HE IDEA OF THE SPIRITUAL JOURNEY is referred to by St. Paul (1 Cor 10:1-4) when he wrote,

...our fathers were all under the cloud and all passed through the sea; by the cloud and the sea all of them were baptized into Moses. All ate the same spiritual food. All drank the same spiritual drink (they drank from the spiritual rock that was following them, and the rock was Christ).

This desert itinerary was also used by Origen (185-254 A.D.), who was struck by the stages of the Israelite's desert journey in chapter 33 of Numbers.

The following are the stages by which the Israelites journeyed up by companies from the land of Egypt under the guidance of Moses and Aaron... (Nm 33:1).

He extensively used this as an analogy to the stages of the pilgrim's itinerary toward coming closer to God, in his treatise, *An Exhortation to Martyrdom, Prayer, First Principles: Book IV*. He saw the spiritual itinerary of the pilgrim soul to take place in stages in a desert experience in the soul, as in the crossing of the Reed Sea (Baptism) and the wandering sojourns of the Exodus.

Later, other spiritual writers, even to the present day, have used the desert journey with its stages as a paradigm of the pilgrim's itinerary. The seven sacraments have been seen as stages or markers on the way in a sacramental spirituality. We see this explicated in the *Catechism of the Catholic Church* (#1210):

> The seven sacraments touch all the stages and all the important moments of the Christian life: they give birth and increase, healing and mission to the Christian's life of faith. There is thus a resemblance between the stages of natural life and the stages of the spiritual life (Libreria Editrice Vaticana, 1994: p.311).

We in the Church are described as a "Pilgrim People," emphasizing the communal character of our Christian journey, through the pronouncements of Vatican Council II:

> What the council underscored is that as an assembled people, understood both actually and historically, we are on the way, whether we are popes or peasants, poor or rich, lay or cleric, toward a final goal which is at the end of history. All are called to a common journey because all have undertaken a common baptism (Cunningham, 1996: pp.49-51).

Before treating the specific stages of some spiritual writers, we should describe the grades, or degrees, of perfection along the way in which they are in context.

A. GRADES OF PERFECTION

Traditionally, spirituality has been perceived by early spiritual writers to be divided into three ways, degrees, or grades of perfection. Pseudo-Dionysius (ca. 500 A.D.), the Areopagite, called the divisions: purgative, illuminative, and unitive. Correspondingly, St. Thomas Aquinas, and later St. John of the Cross, described these states as: beginners, proficients, and the perfect.

It has even been observed from Scripture by several writers that the Apostles, who were mentored by Jesus Himself, had undergone three states in their own interior spiritual life which were distinct and punctuated by progressive conversions. The first, that of beginners, proceeds from their initial conversion to the Passion of Jesus, wherein the Apostles reestablished themselves after their abandonment of Him and Peter repented of his three denials. The second, that of proficients, moves from this second conversion (or dark night of the passive purification of the senses) after the Passion, to Pentecost, in which they were illumined, given courage, and fired with zeal. This state ended with the painful loss of the corporal presence of Jesus upon His ascension to heaven. They were left to live by sheer faith and to face the persecutions promised to them as their lot. The third, that of the perfect, was initiated by a passive purification of the spirit, wherein they were transformed spiritually, bringing them into the perfect life.

They enjoyed a more profound union with God in this state and a spirit of abandoned self-immolation. Consequently, they were impelled to preach openly without fear and to face martyrdom with courage (Garrigou-Lagrange, 1947: pp.225,229-230).

Thomas deVallgornera, in his treatise *Mystica theologia divi Thomae* (1662), writes of some spiritual authors who have embellished on "the characteristics of the three ages of the spiritual life":

1) The purgative way or stage, proper to beginners, in which it is a question of the active purification of the external and internal senses, of the passions, of the intellect, and of the will, by mortification, meditation, prayer; and finally, it is a passive purification of the senses... by means of which the soul is raised to the illuminative way, as St. John of the Cross says.

2) The illuminative way or state, proper to proficients, in which.... are discussed the gifts of the Holy Ghost... which proceeds principally from the gifts of understanding and wisdom... as being morally necessary for the full perfection of Christian life. This second part of the work, after several articles relating to extraordinary graces (visions, revelations, interior words), ends with a chapter of nine articles relative to the passive purification of the spirit, which marks the passage to the unitive way. This again is what St. John of the Cross taught.

3) The unitive life or stage, proper to the perfect, in which it is a question of the intimate union...

with God and of its degrees up to transforming union (Garrigou-Lagrange, 1947: pp.226-227).

References to contemplation in the above have not been included so as to reflect the view of Scaramelli, S.J. (1687-1752 A.D.), in his work *Direttorio mystico,* in which he treats of infused contemplation as an extraordinary grace. This is not to say that infused contemplation is precluded from or not considered by others as ordinary to the spiritual life.

Marguerite Porete (Babinsky, 1993: pp.136,137ff) tells us that before we arrive at spiritual perfection (divine life), it is necessary that the soul dies three entire deaths: 1) the death to sin; 2) the death to nature; and, 3) the death to the spirit. These three transitions correspond to passages to each of the purgative, illuminative and unitive states mentioned before. They each give birth to higher modes of life successively along the way. The three deaths parallel the *dark nights* of St. John of the Cross. After conversion from sin (death to sin), the dark night of the senses is the death to nature, while the dark night of the spirit is the death to the spirit.

The first death, to mortal sin, ushers in the state which embraces the life of grace. It begins with the commandments and reliance on God's help—particularly, observance of the greatest command of all necessary for salvation: to love God above all and one's neighbor as oneself. This life of grace is one of ordinary believers which is minimally sufficient for availing of salvation, yet dismally short of living the noble divine life. Souls in this category are not privileged to the divine secrets of the hidden (mystical) life, and are far from possessing divine Love, called *Fine Amour* by Porete.

The second death, to nature, beckons the soul to live the life of the spirit. The devout soul pursues the counsels of evangelical perfection in accordance with one's state in life. It lives in obedience to the virtues and in accordance to the Beatitudes. We must die to this life of the spirit before reaching the sublime state of living the divine life in *Fine Amour* (divine love).

Divine life cannot be attained until the death of the life of the spirit, no matter how spiritual it is, because the soul is still in possession of its will (although conformed to the divine will) distinct from God's will. So it is not only necessary to die to the spirit, but the will must be abandoned by the soul, thereby giving God permission to consummate its annihilation. Of this event, which Meister Eckhart calls "Durchbruch"—breaking through of the soul to the Godhead—he says powerfully, "For us to give ourself to God is… to give Him absolutely nothing; but for God to take the self, is for Him to take absolutely everything" (Roberts, 1993: p.210). This annihilation of the will, which can only be wrought by God, brings the soul from the former state reached in the life of the spirit of distinct union (*unitas distinctionis*) to the sublime state of indistinct union (*unitas indistinctionis*). In distinct union, the soul wills what God wills. In the indistinct union, there is only God's willing in the soul with His will, since the will of the soul has been annihilated.

It appears that Martin Buber, the respected Jewish philosopher of our time and a scholar of Hasidism and the Jewish religious tradition and theology, has this to say of this state:

Now from my own unforgettable experience I know well that there is a state in which the bonds of the personal nature of life seems to have fallen away from us and we experience an undivided unity. But I do not know—what the soul willingly imagines and indeed is bound to imagine (mine too once did it)—that in this I had attained to a union with the primal being or Godhead.... I can elicit from these experiences only that in them I reached an undifferentiable unity of myself without form or content.... This unity is nothing but the unity of this soul of mine, whose *ground* I have reached, so much so, beneath all formations and contents, that my spirit has no choice but to understand it as the groundless (Buber, 1947: p.43).

Paul, too, seems to allude to having arrived at this state of living the divine life:

It was through the law that I died to the law, to live for God. I have been crucified with Christ, and the life I live now is not my own; Christ is living in me. I still live my human life, but it is a life of faith in the Son of God, who loved me and gave himself for me (Gal. 2:19,20).

B. STAGES OF THE JOURNEY

Spiritual writers such as St. John of the Cross, St.Teresa of Avila, and Marguerite Porete have written of stages of the spiritual journey manifested in degrees of prayer within the concepts of the three grades of perfection: beginners (purgative), proficients (illuminative), and the perfect (unitive).

These stages are identified to map out the pathways, the thresholds of significant spiritual advances, and the milestones of conversions which are commonly (not by all nor in the same way) experienced by spiritual wayfarers. We believe that since a serious prayer life requires introspection as to our spiritual state, that a map is necessary for the following reasons:

1. To have knowledge of our final destination.

2. For encouragement, support, and assurance.

3. To provide a means to recognize *oases for imbibing the waters of Siloe* where we receive God's spiritual favors, graces, and communications.

4. To know how we should act during, and in accordance with, the stages of development.

5. To provide a way of perceiving spiritual progress and how much closer one has reached the destination.

6. To prepare one for discernment between divine favors and self-deceptions or demonic intrusions.

7. To inform as to what are mature states; and,

8. Having tasted and seeing the goodness of God, a strong impetus is given to persevere through darkness in the light of faith to keep advancing higher toward union.

Knowing the way, therefore, and especially the lofty destination of the life of prayer, spurs us to continue onward without wearying and to make persevering effort to live the life that is its condition (Dubay, 1989: pp.73-76).

One of the main purposes of this book is to familiarize the wayfarer of these stages with not only a map and a description of the way, but also to relate what types and degrees of union are attainable in this life. This is to provide the knowledge and understanding of such possibilities and the encouragement to aspire to entering the sublimest state of union with the Divine short of beatitude here on earth.

Each person is called to follow spiritual pathways unique to his or her state in life, temperament, strengths, etc., which should be followed out of obedience to the Father. Should He lead you along similar roadways to those described in these stages, you may find useful parallels. However, one should not attempt to fit life's journey to them. Cunningham (1996: p.63) quotes a recent spiritual writer on this point:

> However detailed the maps may appear in descriptions of the journey, they are in fact broad outlines offered by our brothers and sisters in the faith. We can learn from them and be encouraged by them. But their teachings are not rigid classifications into which we must fit our life's journeys; they must be filtered through the prism of our own uniqueness and cultures [(Richard Byrne, O.C.S.O., "Journey Growth and Development in Spiritual Life)" in *New Dictionary of Catholic Spirituality* 576].

We must pray that we will reach the level of prayer that God decides He wants us to advance to in this life, remembering that the way to heaven is on the narrow path of crosses and trials.

The best known classification of the stages is given in terms of nine degrees or grades of prayer: (1) vocal prayer; (2) meditation; (3) affective prayer; (4) prayer of simplicity; (5) infused recollection; (6) prayer of quiet; (7) prayer of simple union; (8) prayer of conforming union (espousal prayer); and (9) prayer of transforming union (spiritual marriage) or *unio mystica*. This classification has been used, for the most part, by St. John of the Cross, at least implicitly. It was adopted by St. Teresa of Avila, Rev. James Alberione (S.S.P., S.T.D.), and Rev. Reginald Garrigou-Lagrange (O.P.) more explicitly in their works (see Appendix A). St. Teresa of Avila gives us the clearest description of these within the context of her "seven mansions" in her book *The Interior Castle* or *Mansions*. An abbreviated description is given by Alberione (1978: pp.9,10) as follows:

> The first degree of love of God is *vocal prayer,* which teaches us how to speak with God.
>
> The second degree is *meditation,* which causes us to contemplate [reflect on] God's perfections.
>
> The third degree is *affective prayer,* which St. Teresa of Avila describes as "prayer more of the heart than of the mind, in which the affections of the will dominate the reasoning of the intellect."
>
> The fourth degree is *prayer of simplicity*, which consists in a simple, loving gaze upon God Himself....
>
> The fifth degree, *infused recollection,* is a most vivid light that God gives to the soul. This... captivates the intellect.

The sixth degree is *prayer of quiet,* "in which" writes St. Teresa, "the soul feels the presence of God and is lost within it, inebriated with love, revelling in the joy that it no longer lacks anything."

The last three degrees: *prayer of union, prayer of ecstatic union,* and *prayer of transforming union,* belong to the mystic life and constitute the complete divinization of man.

A lesser known classification of the stages of the spiritual life is given by Marguerite Porete (Babinsky, 1993: p.189ff) in her chapter 118. Prior to describing these stages of Porete, a brief exposition of her cultural and spiritual world and environment in the Middle Ages is appropriate. This is a spiritual period which Bernard McGinn (1998) calls the *New Mysticism.*

It is thought that Porete might have belonged to a group of semi-religious women called *mulieres sanctae,* or "beguines," in the thirteenth century. However, little is known of her life. She does not claim to be a beguine and even seems somewhat chiding of them at one point in her writing. It appears that if at one time she had been one, she may not have been at the time she wrote her book *The Mirror of Simple Souls.* Notwithstanding this, her spirituality seems to have evolved from this school which, according to her writings, took her beyond that of former mystics like Hildegard.

The beguine movement had its origins in the area of the old Carolingian Empire called Lotharingia. It began in the lowland region of Belgium, and spread to the Rhineland, even into France and Holland. Its central charisms, besides prayer and service, were an avid love of God (called *minne*) in a relentless pursuit of Him, and living the apostolic life (*vita apostolica*)—the life of Christ and the Apostles. It was alive in northern Europe predominantly around Liege until the time of the French Revolution. At first, it consisted of scattered "holy women" (*mulieres sanctae*) leading very holy lives while still in the secular world. Then, fearing that the beguines were about to form local communities on their own recognizance, the Church intervened to put them under its authority and guidance by assigning them to existing orders (mainly Franciscans, Dominicans, and Cistercians). Next, they formed enclosures under the guidance of these orders because of their work of service in infirmaries and hospices. Lastly, the beguines organized themselves into parochial enclosures:

> The full-blown beguinage comprised a church, cemetery, hospital, public square, and streets and walks lined with convents for the younger sisters and pupils and individual houses for the older well-to-do inhabitants. In the Great Beguinage at Ghent, with its walls and moats, there were at the beginning of the fourteenth century two churches, eighteen convents, over a hundred houses, a brewery, and an infirmary (Petroff, 1994: p.54).

The associated male counterparts were called "beghards." In the early half of the fourteenth century, the religious women (*mulieres religiosae*), as the beguines were known, had gained the admiration and interest of nearly all ranks of clergy, and especially by Dominican friars. Indeed, these friars were so convinced of their holy way of life that they not only encouraged them, but also gave them spiritual guidance. This was exemplified by the career of the Dominican Thomas of Cantimpre.

The fervor of these women (*mulieres religiosae*), distinctive to the *New Mysticism* of the time, gave rise to what Richard of St. Victor calls "the insanity of love" (*insania amoris*). This was also called *violenta caritatis*, violent love. Concerned with disinterested love, which is simple and pure, they were convinced that true love of God manifests itself in vehemence or violence.

The beguines, like Hugh and Richard of St. Victor, stressed the primacy of love over the intellect (*amor ipse intellectus est*). Love becomes knowledge; it alone is able to fathom the profundity of God which transcends all intellectual inquiry. In their Christian "knowing" they were able to embrace the doctrine of "unity of spirit" (*unitas spiritus*) with God. They sought the infinite progress of the itinerary to union that can never exhaust the depths of God (*epektasis*). Here we must emphasize that they placed great importance to Eucharistic mysticism in the Cistercian tradition held by William of St. Thierry.

The idea of union of spirit has its basis in 1 Corinthians 6:17; NASB, *"But the one who joins himself to the Lord is one spirit with Him."* This union is traditionally that understood to be *unio mystica* (mystical union). In the beguine Hadewijch, we see one of the earliest of those in western mysticism who gives rise to the *New Mysticism* of the beguines. She moves beyond *unio mystica*:

> The Dutch beguine moves beyond conceiving of union with God as a loving union of finite spirit with Infinite Spirit (*unitas spiritus*) to a deeper

and more daring treatment of union involving something similar to the *unitas indistinctionis* (union of indistinction) found in Eckhart and other late- thirteenth- and fourteenth-century mystics…. We should not seek in Hadewijch any systematic account of such a theology of union (this would involve the dubious category of "Wesenmystik" that has sometimes been applied to her) (McGinn, 1998: p.217).

"Then it was to me" [Hadewijch], she says, using one of the later technical terms for such a union, "as if we were one without distinction." These and other texts clearly move beyond twelfth-century expressions of mystical union toward the indistinct union favored by some late-thirteenth-century mystics like Marguerite Porete and Meister Eckhart (McGinn, 1998: p.218).

Parallel to the beguines' mysticism of Love, traditionally known as *minnemystik,* we note another spiritual thrust which helps us understand the full impact of their efforts. This is the mysticism of being called *wesenmystik.* St. Augustine, in urging us to participate in God—"to be in the only real Being" (*wesenmystik*), insists that, in such participation, the soul is not a part of the divine substance. William of St. Thierry, in asserting that we must become "what God is," means that "we must become by grace what God is by nature" [*theosis*] (Zum Brunn, 1989: p.xxvii).

Petroff contrasts the minnemysticism of Hildegard against the beguine mysticism:

There is also a [spiritual] theological difference between the beguine mystics and the mystics, like Hildegard, who preceded them. According to Zum Brunn and Epiney-Burgard, in Hildegard's writings "the soul, at the summit of the vision, becomes similar to God," while for the beguines "the soul is annihilated to 'become what God is'" (Petroff, 1994: p.12).

Dom Porion, in an introduction to translations of works of Hadewijch and Beatrijs, notes the most striking characteristic of beguine mysticism to be

...the inner orientation, the impetus which urges the soul to overpass herself in order to be lost in the simplicity of the Divine Being (Petroff, 1994: p.12).

It is worthwhile to quote Bernard McGinn, who adroitly describes the advance of mysticism in the late middle ages:

Many late medieval mystics seemed to have abandoned the notion of the *ordo caritatis,* the restoration of the proper harmony between love of God and all other loves, in favor of what might be described as a new form of *epektasis,* that is, an infinite and *insane* pursuit of God, one based on an overpowering love that is subject to no law but itself and able to find no term but its own annihilation.

The madness of love functions, in part, to break down the ordinary boundaries of consciousness and selfhood. Infinite longing reveals that the soul or self is in some mysterious way

itself infinite, so that the annihilation of the created will leaves nothing present but God, or
rather, the "No-thing" or "No-self" that is the
most adequate way to point toward the true God
who lies beyond the God of limited human
thoughts and aspirations (McGinn, 1998: p.157).

In the state of annihilation (of the will), the soul lives
"without a why," a term encountered for the first time in
a small book by Beatrijs, *The Seven Manners of Love*.
"Living without a why" refers not only "to the gratuitous
nature of divine Love, but also to the total detachment of
the annihilated soul" (Zum Brunn, 1989: p.xxxi). Of this
mode of living, Marguerite Porete says that the soul is
reduced to a nothingness that gives her everything:

She "swims and bobs and floats" in divine peace
[*quies*] and fruition "without any movement in
her interior and without any exterior work"
(McGinn, 1998: p.264).

Eckhart says that whatever limits our mystical
knowledge of the divine Transcendence may reach,
something of Him will always remain beyond our grasp.
Our greatest joy abides in this (Zum Brunn, 1989:
pp.xxxii,xxxiii).

Lamprecht von Regensburg says of those beguines
reaching *wesenmystik*: "'Free of themselves and all
things,' they aspired 'to see without intermediary [as do
the Seraphim] what God is'" (Zum Brunn, 1989: p.xxxiv).

Beatrijs, in an attempt to answer the question "what
is *minne* (love)?" wrote her treatise *Seven Manners of
Loving*. She begins, "There are seven manners of loving,

which come down from the heights and go back again far above" (McGinn, 1998: p.171).

The seven manners of *minne* of Beatrijs are: (1) an active longing; (2) a total disinterested love; (3) the torture of love; (4) the senses are sanctified in love, the will is turned into love, and the soul is made wholly into love by deep immersion and absorption in the abyss of love (*abyssus caritatis*); (5) love is vehemently excited with fierceness, the heart is wounded again and again (*vulnus amoris*); (6) the conflict between love and all human modes of knowing is overcome wherein the soul reaches a condition of closeness to God that allows her to experience divine power, purity, sweetness, and freedom as well as gaining "intimacy" with God (*fraumystik*); (7) a deep desire (unaware of what) to attain the fruition of *minne* (to overpass *minne* to reach *wesen*) through pain and joy—an *epektasis* of *minne*. The soul longs for death and refuses all consolation, even from God. She is drawn into the eternity of *minne,* its sublimity, and the deep abyss of the Godhead in a new concept of *unitas spiritus* or *unio mystica* (McGinn, 1998: pp.171-173).

Beatrijs exemplifies the important aspects in the shift from the mysticism of the twelfth century (*unio mystica*) to that of the thirteenth century; especially, in the move from the language of *caritas* to that of *minne* (eventually leading to *wesenmystik*) (McGinn, 1998: pp.173-174).

Hadewijch identifies *minne* with God Himself, following the biblical text of 1 John 4:16 *"God is love"* (*Deus caritas est*):

The power which I come to know in the nature of "minne"

Throws my mind into bewilderment:
The thing has no form, no manner,
no outward appearance.
Yet it can be tasted as something actual:
It is the substance of my joy.

O powerful, wonderful minne,
You who can conquer all with wonder!
Conquer me, so that I may conquer you,
In your unconquered power
(McGinn, 1998: pp.201-202).

Hadewijch often discusses the exemplary existence of the human individual in the eternal Being (*Wesen*) of God (McGinn, 1998: p.214). She maintains that ecstatic experiences are not as essential to mystical consciousness as the recognition of God's presence despite His apparent absence, the awareness that in the midst of suffering we may find joy, and hidden in *unfaith* is an adherence to faith. The fruition and frustration of *minne*, called *epektasis* by Gregory of Nyssa, and the constant advance in unfulfilled-fulfillment, is expressed by Hadewijch,

Inseparable satiety and hunger
Are the appanage of lavish "minne,"
As is ever well known by those
Whom "minne" has touched by herself
(McGinn, 1998: p.220).

She echoes William of St. Thierry's adhesion to God's will in becoming one with Him in all that He Himself is, when she wrote,

When the soul has nothing else but God, when she has no other will than that of God alone, and when she is brought to naught and wills all that God wills with His will, when she is engulfed in Him and reduced to nothing—then He [here Christ] is raised above the earth and draws all things to Him and the soul thus becomes with Him all that He Himself is (Zum Brunn, 1989: pp.108-109).

Friar David of Augsburg seems to bring us to the point of transition to *wesenmystik:*

There the soul is so united with God, that she is what God is, although she is not God—yet one heart, one will, one love, one spirit with God—not only with the union by which she thereupon wills only what God wills, but that she cannot will otherwise than God does (McGinn, 1998: p.116).

Jacopone da Todi (ca. 1236-1306), a Franciscan friar, was a contemporary of Marguerite Porete, but she was unknown to him. He was very explicit in his book *Lauds* in expressing themes of annihilation, nothingness, and the abyss of God and the soul. These he shared with Porete in the *wesenmysticism* of the *New Mysticism* of the beguines and beghards. His writing is in exquisitely poetic form. In treating the relation of annihilation and love, his poetry reaches its epitome in Lauds 90 to 92, in three lengthy poems. These explore divine love as excessive, ecstatic, and annihilating:

Laud 90... concentrates on the violence of the love that has conquered both God and man. Laud 91 describes the union with God attained through such love, emphasizing the annihilation that leads to a state of sinlessness. Finally, Laud 92 (in different poetic form) sets out three stages in the path to self-annihilation. Jacopone's daring formulations regarding overwhelming love, divine nothingness, and a state of sinlessness beyond all willing suggest interesting comparisons with Angela of Foligno (whose work he may well have known), as well as with the French beguine, Marguerite Porete, with whom he could not have been familiar. These shared themes point to a set of issues about the possibility of attaining a form of indistinct union with God characteristic of much late-thirteenth- and early- fourteenth-century mysticism (McGinn, 1998: pp.127-128).

The love expressed in Laud 90 is Christocentric. In willing to give up all, the soul is led by this love to transformation in Christ. This brings the soul to mystical death. The emphasis in Laud 91 is on the "Nothingness" (*alta nichilitate*) wherein the soul becomes identical with God.

To attain this hidden God, human powers have to cease to function and all values need to be reversed as we are raptured into the annihilation of love.

Two other motifs in this challenging poem [Laud 91] are also reminiscent of the language of Marguerite Porete in... *The Mirror of Simple Annihilated Souls*. Jacopone insists that in order to arrive at this highest state the soul needs to get beyond all willing: "Both willing and not willing are annihilated in you." This implies that our created will must become nothing in order to be merged into the divine *nihil* in some form of indistinction. In such a state the soul wills without a will, desiring nothing and possessing no power in itself (McGinn, 1998: pp.129-130).

Laud 92, on deep union, "distinguishes three stages on the path to annihilation": (1) utter renunciation of the will; (2) divesting of wisdom by the intellect, since it is not capable of swimming in the sea of love (reflecting the necessity for the intellect to yield to love for the final advance into God); (3) a final state of a combination of expressions "of both pain and tranquil rest in God (quies)" (McGinn, 1998: pp.130-131; Hughes, 1982: pp.257-278).

As with Mechthild, Tauler, Ruusbroec, Hilton, and Julian of Norwich, the theme of mystical annihilation was tantamount even more forcefully in Marguerite Porete. This core theme gave impetus to the daring quality of these late medieval mystics. However, Marguerite in her *Mirror* exceeds these writers in the direct, compelling passion of her longing for her Lord (Crawford, 1990: p.12).

Marguerite was a visionary of Hainault (Belgium). Her book had been circulated within a century of her demise in Latin with several vernacular translations. The work was ascribed to a Carthusian monk, which accounted for its acceptance and admiration, in an age when it would be suspect coming from a lay woman. This ironic twist accounts for the survival of her work to the present day. Indeed, it is a great tribute to it that it became a staple of devotional reading (*lectio divina*) in convents and monasteries throughout the continent of

Europe for over 600 years. Fifteen manuscript versions are still extant.

In 1946, to the delight of many, especially women, Marguerite's work became indisputably accredited to her again by Romana Guarnieri (Murk-Jansen, 1998: p.76; Crawford, 1990: p.10).

Marguerite's seven stages are to be taken in context with her three degrees of perfection, or three deaths, in the "movement from grace through the spirit to the life of unity in God" (McGinn, 1994: p.80). This is her second effort to reveal her spiritual teaching of annihilation:

> Marguerite actually makes two attempts to convey her doctrine of annihilation. The first is stageless and ateleological. One is not on a journey or climbing the steps of a ladder as in St. John Climachus' influential *Ladder of Perfection,* but only present before the mirror. Near the beginning of her treatise, she describes the soul in terms without projects or stages, "No one can find her; she is saved by faith alone [because now God does His works in her]; she is alone in love; she does nothing for God; she leaves nothing to God; she cannot be taught; she cannot be robbed; she cannot be given anything; she has no will" [*Mirouer,* chap. 29 (McGinn, 1994: p.80)].

McGinn (1994: pp.80-82) briefly describes some essentials of Porete's seven-stage effort:

> From keeping the commandments to imitating Christ in the counsels of perfection, she accomplishes the works of goodness in the first

three states, but she is so attached to doing
these works that the will must then be put to
death, martyred, pulverized, "to enlarge the
place where love would want to be, and to
encumber the self by several stages in order to
unencumber the self to attain one's being"
(Babinsky, chap. 118,190). It is at this stage
that the will must begin to be annihilated. The
soul then passes into the embrace of union of
the fourth state where she becomes "so danger-
ous, noble and delicious" that she mistakenly
believes this to be the highest gift God can
give… the soul is, however, greatly deceived.

However, in the fifth stage, the soul begins to
move toward a more essential, ontological union;
the dialectic here is between Being and Non-
Being, God's Being and her not-being without
God. Now, delivered from her own will, standing
in the blinding light of Love, the soul in this state
sees "what God is, that God IS." "The Soul considers that God is Who is, from whom all things
are, and she is not if she is not of Him from whom
all things are" (Babinsky, chap. 118,191: *Mirouer*
324). Her will to love is replaced by the will
"given" her by the God who is Being and an overflowing Goodness, and her own resplendence dis-
appears in the flood of Divine Light poured into
the soul to move her will (*ibid*). She stands
abashed at the sight of God's infinite goodness
giving free will even to her nothingness….

In the sixth state the soul no longer sees herself or God, but rather God sees God in her so

that she sees that none is but God.... At this point the terms of the dialectic disappear into a nothingness that has become All, an all that has become Nothingness. At this final earthly stage, even before the seventh state's heavenly beatitude, the soul, returned to her origins, "is in the stage of her prior being" (Babinsky, chap. 138, 219; Mirouer, 400).

St. John of the Cross teaches us that Love is at the heart of the pilgrim's itinerary. He urges the spiritual itinerant to learn to love Him Who is Love: "Every stage of progress is marked by a greater increase in love for the Beloved" (Poslusney, 1973: p.1).

He also tells us that we must desire "nothing but God" to attain to liberality of spirit and harmony in the highest degree (see Appendix B) (Muto, 1991: pp.36,37):

To reach satisfaction in all
*   desire its possession in nothing.*
To come to possess all
*   desire the possession of nothing.*
To arrive at being all
*   desire to be nothing.*
To come to the knowledge of all
*   desire the knowledge of nothing.*
To come to the pleasure you have not
*   you must go by a way in which you enjoy not.*
To come to the knowledge you have not
*   you must go by a way in which you know not.*
To come to the possession you have not
*   you must go by a way in which you possess not*
To come to be what you are not

you must go by a way in which you are not.
For to go from all to the All
   you must deny yourself of all in all
And when you come to the possession of the all
   you must possess it without wanting anything.
Because if you desire to have something in all
   your treasure in God is not purely your all.
In this nakedness the spirit finds
   its quietude and rest.
For in coveting nothing,
   nothing raises it up
   and nothing weighs it down,
   because it is in the center of its humility.
When it covets something
   in this very desire it is wearied.

"Vanity of vanities," says Qoheleth, "vanity of vanities! All things are vanity" (Eccl 1:2).

"What profit is there for one to gain the whole world yet lose or forfeit himself?" (Lk 9:25).

"Whoever humbles himself shall be exalted" (Mt 23:12).

David's psalm: Happy the man to whom the Lord imputes not guilt (Ps 32:2).

To arrive at being all desire to be nothing [nada] (Kavanaugh, OCD, et al, 1973: p.103).

I was annihilated and knew not (Ps 72:22) (Kavanaugh, OCD, et al, 1973: p.344)

"Eye has not seen, ear has not heard, nor has it so much as dawned on man what God has prepared for those who love him" (1 Cor 2:9).

At the evening of life, you will be examined in love. Learn to love as God desires to be loved and abandon your own ways of acting (Kavanaugh, OCD, et al, 1973: p.672).

Whom have I in heaven but Thee? And besides Thee, I desire nothing on earth (Ps 73:25; NASB).

I die because I do not die (Kavanaugh, OCD, et al, 1973: p.720).

Precious in the eyes of the Lord is the death of His faithful ones (Ps 116:15).

Oh, what blessings we will enjoy in the vision of the Most Blessed Trinity! (Kavanaugh, OCD, et al, 1973: p.682).

CHAPTER FOUR

Ascent to Sublime Perfection

T HE LONGER TITLE OF MARGUERITE PORETE'S work is *The Mirror of Simple Annihilated Souls and Those Who Only Remain in Will and Desire of Love.* It is both a treatise and a sort of handbook. As a treatise, it is written as a Boethian-type dialogue between Reason, Love, and the Soul. This dialogue consists of a debate among these figures on the relationship between the human and the Divine, and in what way this relationship allows for the ascent of the soul to the sublime state of union without distinction. As a handbook, it offers a help to the pilgrim soul to discern what it requires to succeed in living the life of the spirit (Babinsky, 1993: p.27).

In chapter 118 of Porete's work, the soul details an orderly description of the stages of the wandering journey the soul must go through prior to attaining the simplicity and freedom of sublime perfection (Hollywood, 1995: pp.97-98).

Love describes and compares the differences between the seven stages in a dialogue with the soul in chapter 61:

[Love]: I have said, says Love, that there are seven stages, each one of higher intellect than the former and without comparison to each other. As one might compare a drop of water to the total ocean, which is very great, so one might speak of the difference between the first stage of grace and the second, and so on with the rest: there is no comparison. Even so, of the first four stages none is so high that the Soul does not still live in some great servitude. But the fifth stage is in the freeness of charity, for this stage is unencumbered from all things. And the sixth stage is glorious, for the aperture of the sweet movement of glory, which the gentle Farnearness gives, is nothing other than a glimpse which God wills the Soul to have of her glory itself, which will be hers forever. Thus, by His goodness, He makes for her this showing of the seventh stage in the sixth. The showing is born from the seventh stage, which gives the being of the sixth. The showing is so quickly given that [this Soul] to whom it is given has no perception of the gift which is given.

Soul: What is this wonder? says the Soul herself. If I myself perceived when such a gift were given, I would become myself what is given by the divine goodness. The gift will be given to me eternally when my body has left my soul.

The Spouse of the Soul: This is not something she can make happen, says the Spouse of this Soul. I have sent you betrothal gifts by my Farnearness, but no one asks me who this

Farnearness is, neither the works He does nor that work when He showed the glory of the Soul, for one cannot say anything about it save this: the Farnearness is the Trinity Himself, and [He] manifests His showing to her, which we name "movement," not because the Soul moves herself in the Trinity, but because the Trinity works the showing of her glory in this Soul. Of this none know how to speak, save the Deity alone. Then the Soul, to whom the Farnearness gives Himself, has so great an understanding of God and of herself and of all things that she even sees within God through divine understanding. And the light of this understanding takes from her all understanding of herself and of God and of all of things.

Soul: This is true, says this Soul, there is nothing else. And so if God wills that I possess this great understanding, He takes from me and keeps what I understand, for otherwise, says this Soul, I would not possess any understanding. And if God wills that I understand myself, this understanding also He takes from me, for otherwise I would not be able to possess anything of it.

Love: This is true, says Love, Lady Soul, what you say. There is no surer thing to understand, there is no more profitable possession than this work (Babinsky, 1993: pp.138-139).

With this background, we are ready to say something further of the seven stages, called states, in detail:

A. FIRST STAGE

In the first stage, the power of sin is stripped from the soul through the grace of God so that the soul intends to keep, until death, the greatest of all commandments: to love God above all and neighbor as oneself. Indeed, the soul is resolved to do all it takes to keep these commandments no matter what the cost or the length of time; it has died to sin.

Thus the soul becomes unencumbered and not afraid to ascend higher because it has a gentle heart and is *full of noble courage within*. Those with a petty heart lack the love and generosity to advance since they are cowardly and slothful.

The soul moves to the second stage when this state of minimal Christian living is perceived by her to be wanting or inadequate.

B. SECOND STAGE

The second stage is reached when the soul considers and abandons itself to a higher way of life than just keeping what God commands. The soul, at this point, embraces the mortification of nature by following the evangelical counsels of poverty, obedience, and chastity, as applicable to and as consonant with its state in life. This involves the practice of asceticism in regard to concupiscence, and the rejection of the desire for power, riches, honors, and delights—even licit ones—in order to reach as near as possible the perfection of the evangelical counsels as exemplified by Jesus Christ. The soul does all it can to please her Beloved which becomes her main pursuit. Hence, it has no fear of the loss of possessions, lack of human respect, people's words, nor bodily frailties. Since her Beloved has no fear of them, so neither should the soul whom He overtakes.

When the soul, as a result, has died to nature, she is brought into the third stage.

C. THIRD STAGE

In the third stage, the soul is in the affection of the love of the work of perfection and desires to requite God's love by doing good works while nourishing her spirit. In seeking to offer more to her Beloved, she knows she must sacrifice the attachment to doing the good works so dear to her heart. Thereby the soul gives up its own will in lieu of obeying another will, initiating the dying of the spirit. This dying is a self-emptying (*kenosis*) which opens the soul to be enlarged with God's love. The will is here attempting its own destruction, paradoxically, since the soul is still willing with her own will.

There is greater difficulty in this stage than in the prior two stages:

> For it is more difficult to conquer the works of the will of the spirit than it is to conquer the will of the body or to accomplish the will of the spirit. Thus it is necessary to be pulverized in breaking and bruising the self in order to enlarge the place where love would want to be, and to encumber the self by several stages in order to unencumber the self to attain one's being (Babinsky, 1993: p.190).

Spiritual poverty, fasts, prayers, heroic virtue, and ascetic piety marks the soul in this state.

D. FOURTH STAGE

The fourth stage occurs when the soul is rapt into the heights of love and spiritual delights. Blinded by love, the soul erroneously believes that there is no higher state of perfection possible on this earth because of its spiritual inebriation. She rejects any touch that is not born of the pure delight of love.

Many souls reaching this stage, as a consequence, get stuck on this level, tragically deceived by the love it possesses, for there are two more levels much nobler and of unspeakable greatness beyond this. Spiritual delights and ecstatic experiences do not represent the highest perfection.

Some souls perceive that there is "a know not what" beyond this state of union (*unitas distinctionis*), in recognition of their previous deceptions, which can only be wrought by the death of the spirit. This leads them to renounce the will in totally abandoning it to God, which ushers them into the fifth stage.

E. FIFTH STAGE

At the fifth stage, the soul comes to understand that only God is Who Is from Whom everything has existence; while she is not, from whom nothing is. God has given her free will and the soul understands that her will should return to its source, the being of God Who is Being. It is rendered back to God without reserving any part of it for itself.

The soul seeks her annihilation in love by abandoning herself and her will totally until it is consummated by God. He annihilates the will abandoned to

Him by the soul; this annihilation can only be accomplished by Him.

Annihilation marks the death of the spirit. This death is twofold: the death of the will and also of reason. In this state, the soul discovers her perfection and the awesomeness of her new mode of being. She no longer has a will with which to will; but rather, God's will alone wills in her.

The understanding is expanded by illumination from the Divine, reasoning activity is left behind, and the affective power is subsumed by Love:

> The faculties remain, but the transformation of the soul's affective power into divine love means that the soul no longer makes use of the faculties in a human way (Babinsky, 1993: pp.34,35).

> *Love:* Thought has no more lordship in her [the soul]. She has lost the use of her senses—not her senses, but the use. For Love has carried her from the place where she was, in leaving her senses in peace, and so has seized their use. This is the completion of her pilgrimage, and the annihilation by her rendering of her will which is dissolved in [Love] (Babinsky, 1993: p.34).

The soul has fallen from *minne* (love) into nothingness, and without this nothingness she cannot be all. The fall which she rightfully has fallen is so deep that she is unable to ascend from such an abyss. She is content there, and, out of humility, sees she ought to remain here.

In the fifth and sixth stages, when the soul is drawn into the divine Life by the Holy Spirit, "the fullness of divinity is given to the perfect, annihilated soul" (Babin-sky, 1993: p.30), since the substance of God is in a union-contact with the substance of the soul which receives touches of the Divine occasionally and unpre-dictably. These touches are deep, ineffable, intimate mystical experiences which bring incomparable delight. Although they are light and of short duration, they are worth more to the soul than can be described, surpass-ing the sublimest of earthly experiences (Dubay, 1989: pp.45,46).

> The difference between the levels of being [*wesenmystik*] [in] the fifth and sixth stages lies less in the attitude of the soul than in the way in which God is actively present to her. The Soul strains language to its utmost in her attempt to describe the "opening of the aperture" [in the sixth stage] (Hollywood, 1995: p.99).

F. SIXTH STAGE

Having fallen from love (*minne*) into nothingness, an abyss of humility in which she remains gladly in annihi-lation, the soul in the sixth stage no longer sees herself because of this abyss of humility into which she has fall-en. Neither does she see God on account of His supreme goodness. Instead, God sees Himself in the soul by His divine majesty, Who clarifies the soul with Himself, which makes her transparent. So, she sees singly that there is nothing except God Himself Who only Is and from Whom all things exist. He Who Is, is nothing but God Himself. Thus, she does not see according to herself, for whoever sees the One Who Is does not see except God Himself seeing Himself in this very soul by His divine majesty. In this sixth stage, the soul is freed, pure, and clarified from everything—albeit not glorified as yet, for this only occurs at the seventh stage. The soul, in this purified and clarified state, sees neither God nor herself, but God sees Himself of Himself *in* her, *for* her, and *without* her.

> God shows to her that there is nothing except Him. And thus this Soul understands nothing except Him, and so loves nothing except Him, praises nothing except Him, for there is nothing except Him. For whatever is, exists by His goodness, and God loves His Goodness whatever part He has given through goodness. And His goodness given is God Himself, and God cannot separate Himself from His goodness so that it would not remain in Him. Therefore He is what Goodness is, and Goodness is what God is. And thus Goodness sees itself by His goodness through divine light, at the sixth stage, by which the Soul is clarified (Babinsky, 1993: pp.193,194).

When the soul is rapt into this sixth stage, she has an extraordinary spiritual experience of the Father as the Godhead, the source of the Trinity, permeating her very being. It has the distinct character of the Being of the Godhead, or "Farnearness," as Porete characterizes Him. The movement lasts but a fleeting moment, but its impression is unmistakenly that of eternity. It tastes of eternal life and of glory, an ineffable experience which is indescribable. The *flash* or *spark* (movement) is so brief

that the work of the Farnearness is done before the soul
has any perception or awareness of His work. It is only
after, when the soul returns to its fifth stage, that she
receives an appreciation of what was wrought in her
and the peace (*quies*) that remains.

The Farnearness (the unity of the Trinity) is called
a spark in the manner of an aperture and quick closure.
This spark receives the soul in the fifth stage and puts
her in the sixth for the interval His work endures. After
this interval, the soul returns to the permanent fifth
stage. The event confirms the *breakthrough* to the
ground of the soul, (in Eckhart's terms), and the permanent union with the Godhead (*unitas indistinctionis*),
without intermediary, which had been effected in the
fifth stage through annihilation.

The glory perceived is of the heavenly world, a glory
of God to be heaped upon the soul in the next life of
which it is unspeakable and inconceivable. The work of
the Spark in the sixth stage is the fleeting manifesta-
tion of this glory to the beloved soul.

Even though the soul is transformed into divine love
in stage five, and freed of all things, the perfection and
simplicity of that stage cannot be compared to the radi-
ance and ineffability of the sixth stage. The spouse of
the soul, Jesus Christ, gives her this explanation:

This does not hold in her [the free soul], says the
spouse of this soul; I have sent you the betrothal
gifts by my Farnearness, but no one may ask me
who this Farnearness is, nor his works that he
does and works when he shows the glory of the
soul, for nothing can be said of this except: The

Farnearness is the Trinity herself and shows this manifestness to her that we call "movement," not because the Soul moves herself, nor the Trinity, but because the Trinity works in this Soul the showing of her [the soul's/the Trinity's] glory (Hollywood, 1995: pp.99,100).

Porete (Babinsky, 1993: pp.135,136,138), in chapters 58 and 61, explicates the differences between her seven stages and the interaction of the fifth and sixth stages in the following excerpts:

[Reason]: Ah, for God's sake, says Reason, what do these Souls have to give who are so annihilated?

Love: To give? Says Love. Truly, says Love, whatever God has of value. The Soul who is such is neither lost nor sad. Instead, she is in the depths of the fifth stage with her Lover. There nothing is lacking to her, and so she is often carried up to the sixth, but this is of little duration. For it is an aperture, like a spark, which quickly closes, in which one cannot long remain; nor would that soul ever have authority who knew how to speak of this.

The overflowing from the ravishing aperture makes the Soul, after the closing, free and noble and unencumbered from all things. This happens from the peace of the work of the overflowing and the peace lasts as long as the opening of the aperture. After such an encounter, the Soul keeps herself freely at the fifth stage, without falling to the fourth, because at the fourth she has will, and at the fifth she has none. And because at the fifth stage, of which this book speaks, she has no more will—where the Soul remains after the work of the Ravishing Farnearness, which we call a spark in the manner of an aperture and quick closure—no one would be able to believe, says Love, the peace upon peace of peace which the Soul receives, if he were not this himself.

Understand these divine words in a divine manner through Love, hearers of this book! This Farnearness, which we call a spark in the manner of an aperture and quick closure, receives the Soul at the fifth stage and places her at the sixth as long as His work remains and endures. And therefore she is other. But she remains in the being of the sixth stage for a short time, for she is put back at the fifth stage.

And this is not surprising, says Love, for the work of the Spark, as long as it lasts, is nothing other than the showing of the glory of the Soul. This does not remain in any creature very long, except only in the moment of His movement. Thus such a gift is noble, says Love, for He does His work before the Soul has any perception or awareness of His work. But the peace, says Love, from the operation of my work, which remains in the Soul when I work, is so delicious that Truth calls it glorious food. None who remain in desire are able to be fed by it. Such Souls would govern a country if it had the need, and all without themselves.

[Love]: I have said, says Love, that there are seven stages, each one of higher intellect than the former and without comparison to each other. As one might compare a drop of water to the total ocean, which is very great, so one might speak of the difference between the first stage of grace and second, and so on with the rest: there is no comparison. Even so, of the first four stages none is so high that the Soul does not still live in some great servitude. But the fifth stage is in the freeness of charity, for this stage is unencumbered from all things. And the sixth stage is glorious, for the aperture of the sweet movement of glory, which the gentle Farnearness gives, is nothing other than a glimpse which God wills the Soul to have of her glory itself, which will be hers forever. Thus, by His goodness, He makes for her this showing of the seventh stage in the sixth. The showing is born from the seventh stage, which gives the being of the sixth. The showing is so quickly given that [this Soul] to whom it is given has no perception of the gift which is given.

Soul: What is this wonder? says the Soul herself. If I myself perceived when such a gift were given, I would become myself what is given by the divine goodness. The gift will be given to me eternally when my body has left my soul.

Porete's sense of the centrality of the fusion of the height of the divine goodness and the abyss of the soul's alienation in the soul's immediate consciousness of God was the source of her original name for the Trinity, the

Loingprés (FarNear). McGinn (1998: p.256,257) neatly explains this dialectical term and the new life of the soul having fallen from *minne* into *wesen:*

> The term involves the combining of two quali-
> fiers without a substantive, thus suggesting that
> God is not a thing but is better seen as a dialecti-
> cal "relationship," or "presence," one both infinite-
> ly, distant and unknown and for that very reason
> more "here" in its absence. Porete does not try to
> describe or define FarNigh, but she does talk
> about its effect on (or better "in") the *Annihilated
> Soul.* FarNigh is both "ravishing" (ravissable) and
> gentil/nobile in the courtly sense. He (the word is
> masculine) is "very sweet" (tres doulx) in the peace
> and "unencumbering" he brings to the soul. In
> chapter 84 Love describes what happens to the
> Soul after she has been freed in four aspects:

> > Then she falls from this into an astonish-
> > ment, which one calls "pondering nothing
> > about the nearness of the FarNigh," who
> > is her nearest one. Then such a soul, says
> > Love, lives not by the life of grace, or by
> > the life of the spirit, but only by the
> > divine life, freely not gloriously, because
> > she is not yet glorified.

> The action of FarNigh brings the Soul to the
> ultimate identification of created nothingness
> with divine goodness and being, the place where
> she was "before she flowed out from the Good-
> ness of God," as a remarkable passage from the
> end of *The Mirror* describes:

The farness of the [Goodness] is greater
nearness, because she [Soul] knows that
farness in itself more in its nearness,
which [knowing] always makes her to be
in union with his will without the hin-
drance of anything else that might happen to her. All is one for her, without a
why, and she is nothing in such a One.
Then she has nothing more to do for God
than God has to do for her. Why? Because
he is and she is not.

In the light of the traditional monastic view of the
rarity and briefness of the phenomenon of the loving
union of wills (*unitas spiritus*), we might ask if it were
more permanent in Porete's *wesenmystik*. McGinn
(1998: p.265) ventures to give an answer:

Is union a more permanent phenomenon for
Marguerite Porete? The answer appears to be a
paradoxical yes and no. The *Annihilated Soul*
does say that she is "confirmed in nothingness"
(confermee en nient [chap. 80]), and we have
already noted that Marguerite insists that once
a soul reaches the fifth stage or level there is no
slipping back to the lower stages. In that sense,
union is permanent. Nevertheless, it is clear
that the highest earthly stage, the flash of the
aperture or opening of the trinitarian abyss
itself, is brief and rare and thus the height of
union is not an achieved state here on earth but
has a moving, epektetic character like that
found in many Christian mystics. It is in speak-

ing about these flashes of glory from the divine life, as in chapters 58, 61, 80, 117, and 136, where Marguerite comes closest to what some would describe as autobiographical accounts of mystical consciousness, but the rigor of her apophaticism undercuts all attempts to describe "what" merging in the abyss is like, precisely because it is not a what!

In this state of being (*wesen*), Love generates the Trinity in the soul in union with God, a more challenging notion of *unio mystica:*

> This goodness of the Holy Spirit cojoins it [the will] in the love of the Father and of the Son. This conjunction places the Soul in being without being which is Being. Such Being is the Holy Spirit Himself, who is Love from the Father and from the Son. Such Love from the Holy Spirit flows into the Soul and she is enlarged from the abundance of delights from a very lofty gift, which is given by a spark and majestic juncture from the sovereign Lover, who gives Himself simple, *and makes Himself a simple One* (Babinsky, 1993: p.185).

Adelheid (1312-1375) of Nuremburg, a nun, speaks of the experience of *wesenmystik:* "He [my Beloved] drew my poor sinful soul into the Godhead—a vision that I could never talk about." This causes her to exclaim, "O, you living God, who could deserve something like this, if you did not give it from the freedom of love!" (McGinn, 1998: p.317).

G. SEVENTH STAGE

The seventh and final stage belongs to beatitude in heaven, which awaits the soul and known only on its departure from the body. It cannot even be described it is so exalted:

The seventh stage Love keeps within herself in order to give it to us in eternal glory, of which we will have no understanding until our soul has left our body (Babinsky, 1993: p.194).

A fleeting perception of this glory is given to the soul in the sixth stage, emanating from the seventh, of duration and intensity sufficient to impart knowledge of it, but not to linger long enough to render it the satisfaction proper to eternal life.

H. UNION WITHOUT DISTINCTION (*UNITAS INDISTINCTIONIS*) — *WESENMYSTIK*

In moving from the traditionally known *unio mystica* (mystical union), called "Geburt" or "birth of the Son in the soul" by Eckhart, to the breakthrough into *wesenmystik* (Porete's fifth and sixth stages), which Eckhart calls "Durchbruch" or "breaking through of the soul to the Godhead," only these two events are pronounced and distinguishable in time. All other spiritual experiences and manifestations, such as the loss of the will; the attenuation of other faculties of intellect, reason, memory, and imagination; and the stilling of the passions and emotions are ontological progressions difficult to situate temporally. During the period between *unio mystica* ("Geburt") and the breakthrough ("Durchbruch"), known as *unitas distinctionis* (union of distinction), the soul's will is distinct from God's will yet conforms to His will. This is a period of total self-abandonment of the soul and appears to be one of challenge of the will and its resolve for its (only implicitly and vaguely perceived) eventual state of annihilation. It is a period of violent love or *minnemystik*. Then, after this period of abandonment, the will is annihilated only by the action of the Divine. His will becomes the will of the soul in *unitas indistinctionis* (unity of indistinction) whence love mysticism (*minnemystik)* yields to being mysticism (*wesenmystik*).

There is no mistaking this annihilation, particularly of the will, because, although it seems progressive, it is a pronounced experience of a new state of being. It is a state of knowing permanence and inexpressible profundity impossible to preconceive or imagine prior to its occurrence. The soul is overcome by the awesomeness of such a gratuitous sublime gift of which it deems itself abjectly unworthy.

1. Minnemystik State

In the *minnemystik* period, paradoxically,

time seems like an eternal now, in which all time collapses into a single "now" ....things seem eternally "new" (Forman, 1991: p.153).

The soul lives in the present moment because it is the same as living in eternity.

Manifested in her is a sense of oneness accompanied by a certain depersonalization, a dissolution of boundaries between other persons (as in the communion of saints in

Christ), and an expansion of cosmic consciousness of all creation, yet within the nearness of her being.

The soul finds itself acting "without a why" (Hollywood, 1995: p.116). She responds to the Holy Spirit's promptings, the demands of charity, other presentiments of what to do at appropriate times, and to doings due to the calling of her state in life. Responses rely less on rational justifications, while a sense of will-lessness and passiveness result from losing conscious control in doing God's will. She becomes detached, uninvolved, and not given to emotional display, even of intense feelings. Notwithstanding this, the soul feels rejuvenated, free, and transformed, entering into a new ease and tenderness of life. The sweetness of the love of Christ wells up through the power of the Holy Spirit, and the overflow of love wells up so that she is wont to be forgetful of self and hopes for dissolution into God. This experience is ineffable.

In this expanded reflective consciousness,

> There is one knowing: my knowing God and God knowing me. Elsewhere, the reborn soul is said to know itself "with God's knowing." That is, the soul is self-aware from within the expanded "oceanic feeling" (Forman, 1991: p.164).

Further mystical experiences, insights, and spiritual awareness manifested in the *minnemystik* period are:

- One's life is no longer one's own, but Christ now lives in it
- Experience of Love's two aspects of perception: burning embers and the leaping up of living flames

- Decreased fear replaced by awe of God
- Increasingly seeking to employ the very elusive virtue of humility
- Increased conviction of being a sinner
- Living a life of sheer faith without certitude
- More and more, following an apophatic journey through faith
- A stilling of the passions over time—bodily sensuality removed
- One's soul being stripped from the body
- Intellectual vision of the Trinity residing deeply within the soul
- Deepening of the desire to have a perfect and permanent union with God, and seeking to overpass oneself
- Absence of feelings of grace even after reception of the Sacraments
- A sense of being confirmed in grace while guilt is not imputed (see Rom 4:7,8)
- Loss of savor for anything that is not of God
- Abandonment of one's own way of acting
- An understanding that in the evening of life we will be judged on how much we have loved.

2. *Wesenmystik State*

In the state of *wesenmystik,* Eckhart, in the breakthrough ("Durchbruch" into *wesenmystik*) to the oneness of the Godhead, speaks of a new form of life in terms of a new relationship with the world, the self, and one's actions (Forman, 1991: p.183). Of the oneness of the Godhead we cannot speak; it is so hidden, but it is possible to perceive these new relationships, just referred to above, resulting from the breakthrough.

When this breakthrough comes, the soul's first perception of it is that she has "no will of her own." She cannot will or wish for anything—not even for what God wishes for her. Her will is annihilated, leaving only God's will willing in her. Concomitant to that is an attenuation of the use of the soul's remaining faculties of intellect (reason), memory, and imagination. These remaining faculties are employed for the *doing* of ordinary tasks required for everyday life, carrying out one's duty, and those necessary to satisfy charity. *Doing* takes the place of willing, or life, and being energy—it is effortless (Roberts, 1993: pp.76-77). Divine Love works in and through the soul, according to Porete (Hollywood, 1995: p.116), and she "suggests that the free soul becomes the place in which Love operates" (Hollywood, 1995: p.119).

A unity of all things in God and God in all things are seen. Things lose their individuality and are viewed as formed in simplicity:

> The soul is, embraced by unity.... The unity is the distinction, and the distinction is the unity. The greater the distinction the greater the unity, for that is distinction without distinction (Forman, 1991: 183-184).

The soul is said to have no self. In her treatment of "No-self," Bernadette Roberts (1991: pp.22-23) writes,

As I see it, when Christ said He must go to His Father in order to come to us, He meant that as long as He remained exterior, as an object to be seen, He could not be fully realized within us.... To complete His mission, Christ must subjectively transform and perfect humanity through the invisible work of grace from within, and impart to man His vision of Spirit and Father. Thus, Christ is the most subjective and mystical of all contemplative experiences; gradually, imperceptively, He replaces the subjective self until, in the end, without a self, He is all that remains.

When this dichotomy falls away, God is realized as pure subjectivity, closer than close, the Eye seeing Itself without reflection, a type of "seeing," indescribable and inconceivable.

She states, "that loss of self takes place on a totally mundane level of practical, everyday living" (Roberts, 1991 p.137). She quotes St. John of the Cross in his anticipation of what is beyond the demise of self:

> *I no longer live within myself*
> *And I cannot live without God*
> *For if I have neither Him nor myself*
> *What will life be?*
> *It will be a thousand deaths,*
> *Longing for my true life*
> *And dying because I do not die.*
> (Roberts, 1991: pp.141-142)

Further, Roberts writes on the falling away to *unitas indistinctionis* (*wesenmystik*):

...with the falling away of the union of two, there remains only the clear identity of the One. It seems that for the Rhineland mystics in particular, the final emphasis was not so much on the Trinitarian distinctions in the Godhead as the Trinity's essential Unity or Oneness. This is reflected in our own journey where union with distinction eventually gives way to a unity without distinction—the essential Oneness of the Godhead, that is.

For us to give our self to God is, as Eckhart says, to give Him absolutely nothing; but for God to take the self, is for Him to take absolutely everything (Roberts, 1993: pp.205-206,210).

Karl Ruh, in his formulation of what is distinctive in the beguine spirituality, argues that while Mechthild and Porete stress a love of God that leads to a union without distinction between the loving soul and the divine, for Mechthild this union is always transient as long as one remains in the body.... Marguerite Porete, as Ruh points out, goes farther in appearing to claim that a lasting essential union with the divine can be achieved on earth. Love, in fact, ultimately frees the soul from all desire and servitude, allowing her to become fully united with the divinity.... Important for Porete is that the soul pass beyond its present troubled state to a higher level where "desire" is lost. Having become absolutely humble, the soul loses her "name" and experiences the absolute and constant presence of the divinity.... "He is in my will" (Hollywood, 1995: pp.7-8).

Ellen Babinsky argues that the shift from the fifth to the sixth stages is a movement from union with the differentiated Trinity, manifest as Love (who is feminine), to that with the Father as the undifferentiated ground of the Trinity (Hollywood, 1995: p.100).

CHAPTER FIVE

Sublime State of Divine Union

T HE SUBLIME STATE OF DIVINE UNION, which is the subject of this chapter, involves the treatment of the state of the soul that has reached the most perfect union attainable here in this life, called *unitas indistinctionis* (union of indistinction). This union is one that has overpassed prior unions described as simple union, espousal union, and the transformed union, known as spiritual marriage, *unitas distinctionis,* or traditionally as *unio mystica.*

In this union of indistinction, the soul lives in a state of "being" (*wesen*) with God in a most sublime state which defies expression. With the annihilation of the will, the attenuation of the use of the faculties of intellect and memory, the stilling of the passions, and the diminution of emotional expression, the soul lives in an abyss of nothingness—the nothingness of the soul's being and that of something less than the divine Being. One moment of this nothingness is worth more than years of meritorious works done before reaching this state.

Having experienced the *movement* of the FarNigh, the sublimest contact with the Godhead, the soul is content just to be without being, so co-joined with the Godhead, that being is indistinguishable from Being Itself; although distinct in natures. It is living in the sublime state of life called *wesenmystik*. In this state there is a two-moment union:

> The annihilated soul remains in a union with the Trinity in the fifth stage and from time to time is lifted into her virtual existence in the sixth.... The movement of the Trinity, the power of the unifying oneness of the Persons, lifts the soul into the sixth stage, into her virtual existence in the Father, the One who is true being, the source of all existence. Hence, for the beguine theologian [Porete], the fluidity between the fifth and sixth states reflects the ebb and flow of divinity as Trinity and Unity (Babinsky, 1993: pp.46,47).

Porete says that in *wesenmystik* the soul is in her primordial being, where she was before she was. She is in an abyss of nothingness, neither seeing herself nor God in the depth of her wretchedness which is without bottom. Yet, the soul is content with this state of being. McGinn, (1998: p.263) writes of Marguerite Porete's nothingness in her *Mirror:*

> *The Mirror* uses many metaphors for suggesting the nature of this primordial "unum simplex esse" in which there is no longer any distinction between God and Soul. We have already noted the growing popularity of the language of

the abyss in the thirteenth century, especially among some of the women mystics, like Hadewijch and Angela of Foligno. The abyss is also a favorite term in Marguerite's *Mirror,* appearing more than a dozen times. Reason can address Soul as "O most sweet abyssed one at the bottom without bottom of total humility" (chap. 53) because to be "abyssed in humility and poverty" (see chaps. 23, 38 and 40) is just another way of expressing the annihilation that comes from the Soul's recognition of her total sinfulness. The abyss language is strongest in the description of the fifth and sixth stages of the Soul's journey in chapter 118. Of the fifth stage she says:

> Now such a Soul is nothing…. And so she is all things, for she sees by means of the depth of understanding of her wretchedness, which is so deep and so great that she finds there neither beginning nor middle nor end, only an abyssal abyss without bottom. There she finds herself, without finding and without bottom.

Unlike Hadewijch, Marguerite does not explicitly speak of God as abyss, but her mystical discourse in which the soul attains its own abyss through humility effectively comes down to the same thing insofar as the *anima abyssata* no longer exists but is the nothingness where "she sees neither herself nor him and thus God himself sees only himself by his divine Goodness" (chap. 91).

Such a soul humbles herself to the point of seeing herself as a non-person, because she sees herself as sin, and sin is a non-thing. So she sees herself as doing a no-thing, but God doing everything in her. Such souls have no will or desires—as these are wholly set on God—so that nothing is left but what God wills and desires in them. The soul is beyond spiritual cravings, since she has no desire for anything outside of herself. All this soul longs for is the grace of the Trinity working in her; in this peace of love, all other cares (her sins, sins of others, the transient doing of others, although she is displeased by sin) are not her main concern (charity of course not neglected).

The soul has been deprived of the feeling of grace and of all desires, physical and spiritual.

What do these free souls do without free will? If anyone asks such a soul, "Would you like to be in Purgatory, certain of salvation while in this world?" the soul would answer "No!"

It has no will to want such things, otherwise it would be falling short of love. Its will is possessed by Him Who Is; He knows what is good for it, and it is content with this without any further knowledge, let alone certainty. Knowledge of love is sufficient for it, and this is how it exists. With this knowledge and love dwelling within it, the soul cannot tell good from evil, nor know by itself whether it will be saved or lost.

This soul has been through such mortification, a kenosis, and been so enlightened by grace and dwells so perfectly in the love of God that all bodily lusts have been extinguished in her, as have all spiritual temptations. All passions have been stilled so that they can only be enlisted by deliberation (at age 120 Moses is said by Josephus to know them only by name); there is such a control over them. The soul does not attach such importance to temporal things that it would worry her. Her nature is so well ordered by her closeness to divine love, to which this soul has been united, that she will ask nothing against God's will.

In this state, the virtues now serve the soul instead of the soul serving the virtues.

The soul knows neither shame nor honor, neither poverty nor riches, neither leisure nor cares, neither love nor hate, neither heaven nor hell.

Like the Seraphim whose nature it is to have no intermediary between their love and God's love and to know everything directly through infused knowledge, the soul wants nothing that comes through a go-between.

Therefore, the soul that has become nothing knows all and knows nothing, wills nothing and wills everything. It is not the soul's will that wills, but God's will willing in her. The soul does not take the lead in loving, but lets Love lead and take over her will and have His will of her. So now, Love can work in the soul without the soul's will, and the soul will be free from all cares.

It is a wise soul who is steeped in humility, seeing itself as the worst of sinners. Placing all her hope and trust in the goodness of God has so deadened her that

> ...she is immune to all inner and outer feelings. She can do no more "works," either for God or for herself, [and cannot] concentrate in her prayer; no longer deliberately look for God, or find him within her, or guide herself (Crawford, 1990: p.77).

She is not with herself but where she loves, untroubled in her conscience:

> Such souls have died of love and are no longer conscious of themselves, so they neither desire heaven nor reject hell....
>
> There are few who come through to a life of freedom that never fails,... who have only the will that pure love gives them, since pure love gives one will and one love, one love that is wholly and utterly pure in the state of divine love, always wholly united to the divine will. Those that reach this stage are made nothing, and this matters nothing to them, since they are but God's work and God's work can never be less than everything to them....
>
> The soul becomes herself by becoming nothing, and once she has gone out of herself and become nothing, she has true knowledge of the gifts of God through the miracle of his gift to her, which she receives in faith....
>
> God's goodness is worth more than anyone can do in one hundred thousand years or anything the Church can do in history. The highest point of his goodness is the most accessible, in that it takes the soul into himself and makes her always one with his will, whatever may happen to her. Made one with this one, she is without fear and without joy; she has no more to do for God than he has to do for her, since she is nothing and he is everything. This is enough for her, the fact that he "is"; knowing this, she need hold nothing of herself back in making herself nothing. And nothing she

is: back where she was before she had being. Everything she has is from God and she is what God is [by grace, through participation in transformed love] and was, and what she was before God made her, in union with him....

In this state she can no more pray than she did before she was made, since all she has comes from God's goodness, from the will of his love in the soft dark night. So she cannot pray.... She has held nothing back; she has no space in which to live, and occupying no space, has nowhere to love herself—as is obvious! She is forbidden to work: all she must do is exist in God, become perfectly one with him, as Jesus prayed for His disciples [Jn 14,17 (Crawford, 1990: pp. 77,78; 146-149)].

Clothed in the life of glory the soul is stripped from her body, because, by God's power, her bodily sensuality has been removed. This recalls Psalm 46:10; NJB: *"Be still and acknowledge that I am God."*

The soul lives in the gentle state of surpassing peace and nothing can disturb her—*nothing*. The soul lets the dead bury their dead (Lk 9:60). One needs to be dead to the world and all its lures and attachments to understand this, for otherwise you will not have the life of the Spirit totally in you. If one could only understand how much a moment of this nothingness is worth, its preciousness—how rich one would be!

In the final stage of spiritual being, short of death, called "freedom in enlightenment,"

the soul no longer sees her own nothingness from the depths of humility, nor the greatness of

God through his great goodness. Instead, God sees himself in her through his own power, enlightens her himself, so that she sees that nothing exists save God alone, the source of all being. What is, is God, and the soul sees nothing but God (Crawford, 1990: p.132).

In this sixth stage the soul is purified, enlightened, and free. However, it is not yet glorified; this latter state belongs to heaven and beatitude. Therefore, in this purified and enlightened mode, the soul no longer sees God or herself, but it is God seeing Himself in her. She knows, loves, and praises nothing except Him. "She sees that all is in the being of God... who is love and has paid all debts" (Crawford, 1990: p.133).

Bathed in the flood waters of God's love, the soul swoons and dies of love. The wound of love is the death of reason. Such souls have also died to will and live in a state of death according to the divine will. Being fire themselves, aflame with the pure love of God, these souls are so consumed in this fire of love that they cannot feel the flames. The soul, through its utter humility, is at peace with itself. She loves everything for God's sake, and she loves God in everything. This makes her whole in the pure love of God's love, which is not communicated through the senses, but infused into the soul directly. So clearly does she see that she perceives God in her, not herself in God.

In this soul's being she has an acute awareness of the *mysterium tremendum* attribute of the Deity, a tremendous mysterious otherness of God, a sense of awe, and also taken back by the enormity of His love for each of us.

The annihilated soul is in such a sublime state of union that it no longer feels any joys or even love within herself although she is swimming in a sea of joy and enflamed in the furnace of divine Love. Porete says of this (Babinsky, 1993: pp.107,109),

> *[Reason]:* Now tell me, Love, says Reason, do such Souls feel any joys within them or outside them?

> *Love:* Not at all as regards your question, says Love, because their nature is mortified and their spirit is dead. For all will has departed from them, and on account of this [such a Soul] lives and remains, and is, because of such mortification, in divine will.

> Now listen, Reason, says Love, in order to grasp better your question. That which burns has no cold, and the one who swims has no thirst. Thus such a Soul, says Love, is so enflamed in the furnace of the fire of Love that she has become properly fire, which is why she feels no fire. For she is fire in herself through the power of Love who transforms her into the fire of Love.

> *[Love]:* Such a Soul, says Love, swims in the sea of joy, that is in the sea of delights, flowing and running out of the Divinity. And so she feels no joy, for she is joy itself. She swims and flows in joy, without feeling any joy, for she dwells in Joy and Joy dwells in her. She is Joy itself by the virtue of Joy which transforms her into Joy itself.

In this state, the soul often receives divine "touches" which are extremely delicate and ineffably delightful.

Because they are substantial, they are exceedingly sublime giving a taste of eternal life. St. John of the Cross (Kavanaugh, 1979: p.602) tells us that "the more subtle and delicate the touch, and the more delight, . . . the less volume and bulk it has." He also expresses in what way it is perceived:

> Although that which the soul tastes in this touch of God is not perfect, it does in fact have a certain savor of eternal life, as was mentioned. And this is not incredible if we believe, as we should, that this is a touch of substances, that is, of the substance of God in the substance of the soul. Many saints have attained to this substantial touch during their lives on earth.
>
> The delicateness of delight felt in this contact is inexpressible. I would desire not to speak of it so as to avoid giving the impression that it is no more than what I describe. There is no way to catch in words the sublime things of God which happen in these souls. The appropriate language for the person receiving these favors is that he understand them, experience them within himself, enjoy them, and be silent. One is conscious in this state that these things are in a certain way like the white pebble that St. John said would be given to him who conquers; "and on that pebble a new name written which no one knows, but he who receives it" [Ap 2:17].
>
> Thus one can only say, and truthfully, "that tastes of eternal life." Although one does not have perfect fruition in this life as in glory, this touch, nevertheless, since it is a touch, tastes of

eternal life. As a result the soul tastes here all the things of God, since God communicates to it fortitude, wisdom, love, beauty, grace, and goodness, etc. Because God is all these things, a person enjoys them in only one touch of God, and the soul rejoices within its faculties and within its substance.

Sometimes the unction of the Holy Spirit overflows into the body and all the sensory substance, all the members and bones and marrow rejoice, not in so slight a fashion as is customary, but with the feeling of great delight and glory, even in the outermost joints of the hands and feet. The body experiences so much glory in that of the soul that in its own way it magnifies God, feeling in its bones something similar to what David declares: "All my bones shall say: God, who is like You?" [Ps 35:10]. And because everything that can be said of this unction is less than what it is, it is sufficient to say in reference to both the bodily and the spiritual experience, "that tastes of eternal life" (Kavanaugh, 1979: pp.602-603).

Jordan Aumann, O.P. (1980: pp.342-343), writes of these touches experienced in union:

The "mystical touches" are a kind of instantaneous supernatural impression that gives the soul a sensation of having been touched by God himself. This divine contact imparts to the soul an ineffable delight that defies description. The soul sometimes utters a cry or falls into ecstasy.

The touches themselves admit of varying degrees of intensity; the most sublime are those that St. John of the Cross describes as "substantial touches." The expression designates that the soul senses the mystical touches as if they had been experienced in the very center or substance of the soul, although in reality they are experienced in the spiritual faculties of intellect and will. St. John of the Cross warns souls that they should not attempt to experience these mystical touches by their own efforts but should remain humble and resigned before God and passively receive whatever he deigns to send them.

The soul yearns ardently for eternal life having been purified and having tasted of eternal life. This foretaste, and the impetus of a consuming love, seems to her that she ought to break through the last veil (mortal life) of separation between the soul and eternal beatitude.

When this state is reached, the soul does not pass through purgatory upon its earthly demise:

> The one who reaches such a state, as the Saint [St. John of the Cross] declares explicitly, does not pass through purgatory, and death immediately opens to it the gates of Heaven. The mystical Doctor explains that death itself is caused more by the impetus of love than by natural causes. Even though it may die during an illness or in the fullness of years, the soul is not torn away by these, but by "some impetus or loving encounter more sublime and powerful than

the preceding, which succeeds in tearing away the veil and bearing off that jewel of a soul...."

"Precious in the sight of the Lord is the death of His saints," he had written in the *Living Flame* "because in it are gathered together all the riches of the soul, and into the ocean flow the rivers of its love, which are so swollen and vast that they really seem like seas. Then are united the first and last treasures of the soul so as to accompany it at the moment it is going to depart for its kingdom, while from the farthest confines of the earth resound praises.... which are the glory of the just [*Living Flame I, 30* (Gabriel, 1990: pp.113-114)].

When God invites us to so sublime a union of being with Him, we shrink away and run backward to a more banal or base existence. Because of our human frailties, we are weak and thus easily yield to concupiscence, the Devil's tempting, and the allurements of the world (avarice, greed, egocentrism, etc.). We have a predisposition toward evil which can only be overcome by the grace of God if only we would turn toward Him. Even though our sins be as scarlet, Christ will wash us in His Blood until we are as white as snow. God pursues us unrelentingly with a love beyond telling, and He is ready to shower His graces and gifts upon us when we seek reconciliation with Him. He goes further in giving Himself in union with us. So why do we have so few saints? St. John of the Cross puts it in perspective:

When the Saint thinks that God invites us to such great heights, and we instead run backwards to such baseness, he exclaims: "O souls created for such grandeurs, and called to them! What are you doing? What is detaining you? Your pretensions are baseness, and your possessions are miseries.... Since you are blind to so much light and deaf to such loud voices.... you remain miserable and vile, ignorant and unaware of so many blessings! (Canticle XXXIX, 7)

O souls created for such grandeur and called to it, what are you doing? Oh yes, we too ask ourselves this. We also ask—a little anxiously perhaps—if God truly invites everyone to these heights, so few are the souls that reach them?"

The Saint also in his "Living Flame of Love" (written for a lady who was living in the world) asked himself the question and has not left us ignorant of the reply.

"This happens," he says, "not because God wishes that few be raised to spiritual heights—on the contrary He would like all to be perfect;—but because He finds few subjects capable of enduring so sublime a work" (*Living Flame II, 27*).

The Saint explains that so many souls, when God hardly begins to try them with some inconvenience or temptation, instead of recognizing and accepting it with love, quickly become impatient. They do not wish to suffer; they become disgusted with the way of virtue and return to their natural satisfactions.

"Hence," the Saint continues, and these are the most terrible words he has written, "not finding them strong and faithful in that little.... (the Lord) sees well that they will be much less able to endure greater things, and for that reason He ceases to purify them and to raise them from the dust by means of the labor of mortification, for which a greater constancy and strength is needed than that which they have shown" (*Living Flame II, 27*). With the tremendous consequence that such souls no longer advance and remain buried in mediocrity (Gabriel, 1990: pp.111,112).

Psalm 73:21-28 should give us great encouragement to aspire to the sublime state of the highest divine union possible in this life notwithstanding our sinfulness:

> *And so when my heart grew embittered*
> *and when I was cut to the quick*
> *I was stupid and did not understand,*
> *no better than a beast in your sight.*
>
> *Yet I was always in your presence;*
> *you were holding me by my right hand.*
> *You will guide me by your counsel*
> *and so you will lead me to glory.*
>
> *What else have I in heaven but you?*
> *Apart from you I want nothing on earth.*
> *My body and my heart faint for joy;*
> *God is my possession for ever.*
>
> *All those who abandon you shall perish;*
> *you will destroy all those who are faithless.*
> *To be near God is my happiness.*
> *I have made the Lord God my refuge.*
> *I will tell of all your works*
> *at the gates of the city of Zion.*

(Liturgy of the Hours, Vol. III, 1975: p.1146;
Catholic Book Publishing Co., New York, N.Y.)

St. Francis De Sales also encourages us,

Jesus commanded us to love Him with our whole
mind, with our whole heart, and with all our
strength, and He gives us the grace to do it.
Whoever fails to reach this goal has not lived his
life entirely (Alberione, 1978: p.11).

———— *Part Two* ————

GROWTH IN HOLINESS

One thing I ask of the Lord; this I seek: To dwell in the house of the Lord all the days of my life, that I may gaze on the loveliness of the Lord and contemplate his temple (Ps 27:4).

I sought the Lord, and he answered me and delivered me from all my fears. Look to him that you may be radiant with joy and your faces may not blush with shame (Ps 34: 5,6).

God chose us in him before the world began, to be holy and blameless in his sight, to be full of love; he likewise predestined us through Christ Jesus to be his adopted sons—such was his will and pleasure (Eph 1:4,5).

If anyone is in Christ, he is a new creation. The old order has passed away; now all is new (2 Cor 5:17).

Jesus said to all: "Whoever wishes to be my follower must deny his very self, take up his cross each day, and follow in my steps" (Lk 9:23).

CHAPTER SIX

Advancement in Holiness

A. INTRODUCTION

THIS SECTION OF THE BOOK, PART II, deals with the means and practices for advancement in holiness toward disposing oneself for union with the Divine. It attempts to point the way in a general fashion, recognizing the uniqueness of each individual's pathway to perfection. However, more detailed information may be obtained from the sources listed in the bibliography of this book.

Anyone who wishes to belong to the Lord must first resolve not to commit deliberate serious sin as a minimum—at least, to keep the Ten Commandments with resolve. To advance further to be a faithful disciple and to grow in intimacy with the Lord, the pilgrim soul must live a life in the spirit of obedience, fraternal charity, humility, and detachment, as insisted by Scripture and the Church.

> Because this supreme Beloved demands goodness
> as a condition for intimacy, Scripture insists, just

as St. Teresa does, that we begin by practicing the ordinary virtues with extraordinary fidelity and entirety. We are to walk along a hard road and enter the narrow gate that leads to life. We carry our cross every day (Dubay, 1989: pp.108-109).

We owe obedience to our heavenly Father and to all that our state of life demands. Fraternal charity is the imperative of the commandment to love, and it is a measure of our love of God. It is impossible to live a life of intimacy with the Divine without humility and detachment of the heart from all that is not God. Detachment is required by the admonition of St. Paul in 1 Corinthians 10:31: *"The fact is that whether you eat or drink — whatever you do — you should do it all for the glory of God."*

B. MEANS AND PRACTICES FOR SPIRITUAL GROWTH

In order to attain that goodness and charity required as a disposition for union, not only is purgation (purification) and mortification necessary while observing the commandments, but it is also necessary to put on Christ and grow in His likeness by means of the sacraments, meritorious good works, prayer, and other aids to growth in holiness. We should also be faithful to the Church, which in addition to providing the sacraments and the liturgies for communal prayer, also guides us in faith, morals, and Scripture through its teaching. It shows us the way of the Cross (*via Crucis*), so necessary for the imitation of Christ. The Eucharist is central to growth in the spiritual life.

It is imperative to strive to acquire the theological virtues of faith, hope, and charity, and all the moral virtues covered under the general headings of the cardinal (hinge) virtues; namely, prudence, justice, temperance, and fortitude.

When the soul enters the spiritual journey, she finds herself far from divine union. Usually, there are within the soul, at that time, disordered attachments and appetites of several kinds within her. These inordinate attachments, there in the soul's sensitive nature, are so used to seeking satisfaction in the senses, and hence, inclined to enjoy material pleasures. These inordinate attachments are also present in the soul in its spirit. The soul is thus so full of self-love and complacency of her own excellence that one is the center of the world which it ought to control. It is wont, therefore, to become impatient, discontented, and fundamentally far from humble. It becomes imperative

> ...to purify the sensitive nature and also its spirit from evil and imperfect tendencies and inclinations, which are sometimes very strong and deeply rooted in the soul (Gabriel, 1990: p.33).

This purification requires detachment. That means, *"What we have to do is to give up everything that does not lead to God, and all our worldly ambitions"* (Ti 2:12; JB); it means *everything,* including inordinate affections and desire for anything other than God.

> It is the pure heart that sees God [Mt 5:8], the single-minded person who seeks the things above, not those on earth [Col 3:1-2]. This heart

is sensitized to the Holy Spirit, His enlighten-
ments, movements and enkindlings (Dubay,
1989: p.140; p.326, n.33, n.34).

St. John of the Cross exhorts us to walk in detachment so that God can infuse His love into the will:

> To journey to God, the will must walk in
> detachment from every pleasant thing, rather
> than in attachment to it. It thus carries out well
> the commandment of love, which is to love God
> above all things; this cannot be done without
> nakedness and emptiness concerning them all.
>   God infuses this love in the will when it is
> empty and detached from other particular, earthly
> or heavenly pleasures and affections. Take care,
> then, to empty the will of its affections and detach
> it from them (Kavanaugh, 1979: p.630).

Finally, notes our saint, when the Beloved
sees His beloved empty of all else, He cannot long
stay away. So much does God love us that when
He finds us open and ready, He cannot refrain
from filling us to the extent that we are emptied.
Just as nature abhors a vacuum, so does the Lord
of supernature (Dubay, 1989: p.141).

St. John offers some verses for achieving this single-
minded pursuit through detachment:

> *To reach satisfaction in all*
>   *desire its possession in nothing.*
> *To come to possess all*
>   *desire the possession of nothing.*

To arrive at being all
 desire to be nothing...
For to go from all to the all
 you must deny yourself of all in all
(Kavanaugh, 1979: pp.103-104).

C. AIDS TO SPIRITUAL GROWTH

In addition to the principal means and practices already discussed, certain aids to growth are given here, using the outline and various suggestions of Aumann (1980: pp.358-385), which should prove efficacious:

1. The Presence of God

The practice of the presence of God is the continual recalling that God is present everywhere and in the ground of our soul. It involves the awareness of being in His sight and the salutary effect of one's endeavor to do His will as an added obligatory impetus incurred thereby. This is stressed by Scripture in Genesis 17:1: *"Walk in My presence and be blameless,"* God says to Abraham.

St. John of the Cross says that God is present in us in three ways: by His power, grace and affection. Through His power all things exist and subsist. By His grace we are sanctified. He is in us by affection when we please Him by requiting His love; the more so, the greater our abandonment to Him.

2. Examination of Conscience

The examination of conscience is very profitable for growth in that it calls to mind our failings, faults, and imperfections which tend to distance ourselves from God. This daily examen should be the minimal practiced so as to be consistent. This should lead to more frequent intervals, and eventually to a continual awareness of our actions.

The examination reveals our relationship with God and how far we have progressed in holiness. It presents an opportunity for contrition, resolutions to avoid offense to God, and the practice of virtue.

3. The Desire for Perfection

If we are to reach a high degree of sanctity, we must develop a strong, dedicated desire for it. It is a firm and committed act of the will.

Only energetic and resolute souls will be able to ascend to the summits of perfection.

4. Conformity to God's Will

Attainment of sanctity requires the abandonment of oneself to the will of God and is an excellent spiritual practice. Aumann (1980: p.366) explicates,

> Conformity to the will of God consists in a loving, total, and intimate submission and harmony of our will with that of God in everything he disposes or permits in our regard. When it reaches a perfect state it is known by the name of "holy abandonment to the will of God"; in its less perfect state it is called simply "Christian resignation."

5. Fidelity to Grace

Fidelity to grace means following the promptings and inspirations of the Holy Spirit manifested in us, in whatever form, through loyalty or docility. Response to the Holy Spirit's inspirations involve three aspects:

> Three things are necessary for our response to the inspirations from the Holy Spirit: (1) attention to the inspirations; (2) discretion for distinguishing them from natural inclinations or movements from the devil; and, (3) docility in carrying out the inspiration (Aumann, 1980: p.371).

We should often pray to the Holy Spirit to be enlightened, guided, and strengthened to be faithful to grace and docile to His inspirations and promptings.

6. Plan of Life

A plan of life is the ordering of one's occupations and practices of piety in some schedule commensurate with one's state in life. This is done with the view of providing some constancy and regularity in an effort toward greater perfection

Paramount is: attendance in the liturgy of the Mass, frequenting the sacraments, practice of works of mercy, and the establishment and practice of a regular prayer life, all of which should be dominant in seeking perfection.

7. Spiritual Reading

Spiritual reading, also called *lectio divina,* aids the

practice of prayer and instruction on spiritual doctrine. Most efficacious to this effort is the assiduous reading of books on living the devout life. Such reading tends to renew aspirations of perfection, to strive even greater, and to gain invaluable knowledge about the spiritual journey.

Reading, studying, and meditating on Scripture should take precedence. Next, might be meditation on the life of Christ through the work of Thomas à Kempis titled, *The Imitation of Christ.*

The lives of the saints are a profitable and edifying source of *lectio divina*; especially when selectively chosen. Care must be taken not to give too much emphasis to the extraordinary in the saint's life, lest one attempts to emulate details in the saint's life totally inapplicable to the path the Lord is leading the soul.

The spiritual benefits of spiritual reading are the awakening of one's love of God and the intensification of the soul's desire for sanctity.

It is helpful at times to reread certain sections which continue to be of profit, and to use a book as long as it proves profitable. On the other hand, if a source turns out to be unsatisfactory, one should not feel obliged to waste time reading it from cover to cover, but should select one that is more spiritually profitable .

8. Holy Friendships

A true and holy friendship is a rare gift of God and is to be treasured. It is an alliance of souls seeking goodness. Its marks are: patience, generosity, sincerity, confidentiality, otherness, and disinterestedness. It is neither sensual nor hypocritical. It enables the friends to love each other despite their known and mutually expressed defects. The love in friendship is true charity.

Three prominent advantages that ensue from true holy friendship are enumerated by Aumann (1980: p.378):

> In the first place, a friend can be an intimate confidante to whom one can open the heart and receive advice and counsel when confronted with problems and doubts. Secondly, a friend can be a prudent and sympathetic corrector who will frankly point out one's defects and prevent many acts of imprudence. Thirdly, a friend will console in times of sorrow and will know how to select the proper words and remedies in times of trial.

9. Spiritual Guidance

The art of leading souls progressively from the initiation of the spiritual journey to the summit of Christian perfection is called "spiritual guidance" by this author. It is an art that is distinct from the administration of the Sacrament of Reconciliation.

St. John of the Cross, while eschewing pseudo-spiritual directors, gave us the qualities of a good one. He should be: (1) LEARNED—possessing a thorough knowledge of ascetical and mystical theology and the theological doctrine in regard to Christian perfection; (2) PRUDENT—having prudence in judgement, clarity in counseling, and firmness in exacting obedience; and, (3) EXPERIENCED—having experience in guiding and observing others and the proximate experience in his own spiritual life.

The spiritual guide is in the hands of the principal spiritual director, the Holy Spirit; the guide is merely an instrument. A good spiritual guide will always be cognizant of this fact.

D. CONDITIONS FOR GROWTH

St. Teresa offers us principles or conditions for growth in the spiritual life. She insists on basing her prescriptions for growth on Scripture. Following are nine of her principles which are gathered from her writings:

1. Do God's will from moment to moment throughout the day. She adds that "it is the person who lives in more perfect conformity who will receive more from the Lord and be more advanced on the road."

2. Growth does not depend upon one's immediate situation, for "the time is always propitious for God to grant His great favours to those who truly serve Him."

3. Conformity to the divine will does not mean merely that we fulfill commandments, but also that we generously go beyond what is strictly required. One gives the Beloved everything and anything that will please Him.

4. Development must be accompanied by the purification from faults, for only the pure can commune deeply with the all-pure One.

5. One must make a real effort and not permit pampering of oneself, but embrace the Cross.

It is, after all, a hard road and a narrow gate that leads to life (Mt 7:13-14).

6. Growth is proportionate to our degree of readiness and generosity for it. When these are present in a high degree, the Lord gives much in a short time.

7. Be vigilant against spiritual retrogression. The dangers of retrogression do not appear out of the blue like a flash of lightning. God gives the prayerful person "a thousand inner warnings of the danger."

8. Growth in communing with God requires a correlation between virtue and prayer. This means that the earnest practice of virtue (humility, temperance, patience, love of neighbor, and the like) directly causes a deepening prayer; while as prayer develops, so does one find it much easier to be humble, temperate, patient, and loving.

9. The final fundamental Teresian principle for development is determination. Faintheartedness was not one of her traits. St.Teresa speaks on this principle (Dubay, 1989: pp.112-116):

> It is most important—all important, indeed—that they should begin well by making an "earnest" and "most determined" resolve not to halt until they reach their goal, "whatever may come, whatever may happen" to them, "however hard" they may

> have to labour, whoever may com-
> plain of them, whether they reach
> their goal "or die on the road" or
> have no heart to confront the trials
> which they meet, "whether the very
> world dissolves before them."

E. DISCERNMENT OF GROWTH

Regarding spiritual matters and the judgement of the degree of progress in perfection, people gauging their own development find it elusive and not very straightforward. Most are unrealistic in their evaluation as to whether they are or are not growing in their spiritual lives.

When it comes to the spiritual life, several devout persons assume that good intentions and pious feelings are reliably authentic signs that they are making spiritual progress. In that, they are easily deceived by their limited human faculties, acumen, drives, worldly ways, and demonic influences. Therefore,

> we ought not to imagine that we have achieved
> notable progress simply because we are capable
> of lofty sentiments (Dubay, 1989: pp.235-237).

St. Teresa strongly remarked on this delusion, "O God, what crooked excuses we make and what manifest delusions we harbour!" (Dubay, 1989: p.237). "Sin obscures sight" (Dubay, 1989: p.237), says Hans Urs von Balthasar (the famous theologian), and for this reason saints see right through our merely human evaluations and rationalizations. Their purification was sufficient to equip them with the clear vision to discern their own

previous follies and also our indiscretions and imperfections. St. Teresa admonishes us to doubt what we think
is progressive (Dubay, 1989: pp.237,238):

> More sobering still is Teresa's admonition that we
> do well to entertain healthy doubt about our very
> progress in virtue. One day we appear to ourselves
> invincible, while the next we fall flat on our faces—
> we are far from what we thought we were. The
> saint admits that she is not sure herself when her
> love is spiritual and when it is mingled with mere-
> ly natural emotions, and she agrees with St. Paul
> that demonic deceptions are various and many.

The soul must be humble enough to be open to the
truth; to be receptive and docile to the Holy Spirit in
the discernment of spirits. One should measure spiritual progress more by the perfection of their obedience and diminution of self-willfulness than by felt
spiritual delights.

Jesus' saying *"By their fruits you will know them"*
(Mt 7:20) is one way of discerning growth. We may add
that this applies also to other spiritual and supernatural phenomena. Genuineness of experiences and unusu-
al phenomena must be tested and judged by their good
or evil effects. Sure signs of growth are a love for solitude, a desire to share Christ's sufferings, and the love
of the Cross and the Church.

St. Teresa sums up this subject of discernment as
follows according to Fr. Dubay (1989: p.242):

> We reserve for our last text a statement whose
> closing words are an ideal summation of this

entire chapter: "If any one of you receives high favours, let her look within herself and see if they are producing these effects, and, if they are not let her be very fearful, and believe that these consolations are not of God, Who, as I have said, when He visits the soul, always enriches it." Nothing more need be added.

Appendices

A. THE THREE WAYS OF THE SPIRITUAL LIFE

CHARACTER OF PRAYER	STAGES OR WAYS	DOMINANT MORAL APPEAL	MOVING FROM

Transition: *First conversion or justification—Awakening*

		1. PURGATIVE STAGE (WAY)	D	D	
A			E	I	
C	P	Vocal Prayer	C	M	
Q	R		A	I	F
U	A	Meditative Prayer	L	N	E
I	Y		O	I	A
R	E	Affective Prayer	G	S	R
E	R		U	H	
D			E	I	
				N	
				G	

CHARACTER OF PRAYER	STAGES OR WAYS	DOMINANT MORAL APPEAL	MOVING FROM

[Dark Night of the Senses and Some of the Spirit]

Transition: *Second conversion— Passive Night of the Senses*   **To**

2. ILLUMINATIVE STAGE (WAY)

CHARACTER OF PRAYER	STAGES OR WAYS	DOMINANT MORAL APPEAL	MOVING FROM
M		B	R
Y P	Prayer of Simplicity	E	E A
S R		A	D N
T A	Prayer of Infused Recollection	T	U X
I Y		I	C I
C E	Prayer of Quiet	T	I E
A R		U	N T
L		D	G Y
		E	
		S	

[Dark Night of the Spirit]

Transition: *Third conversion— Passive Night of the Spirit*   **To**

3. UNITIVE STAGE (WAY) (God seems to disappear)

CHARACTER OF PRAYER	STAGES OR WAYS	DOMINANT MORAL APPEAL	MOVING FROM
D O		Love	I
E R			N
I	Prayer of Simple Union	of	T A
F T			E W
I H		God	N E
C E	Prayer of Ecstatic Union,		S
A O	Conforming Union, or Espousal	&	E
T I			
I S		Neighbor	
O	Prayer of Transforming Union		
N	or Spiritual Marriage (individual seems to disappear) (Dawn of the Resurrection)		

B. THE SKETCH OF THE MOUNT—ST. JOHN OF THE CROSS

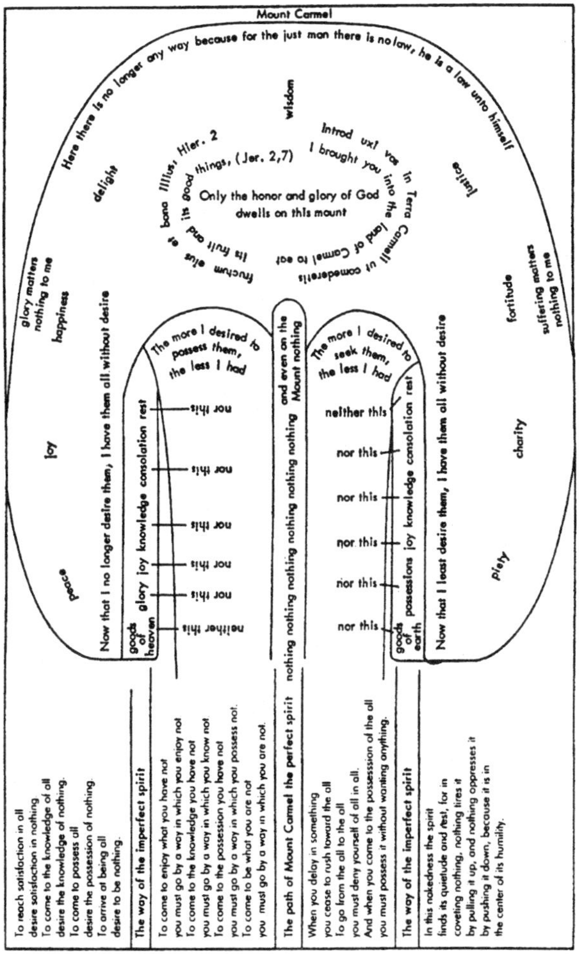

Mount Carmel
Here there is no longer any way because for the just man there is no law, he is a law unto himself
wisdom
delight
justice
Introd uxi vos in Terra Carmeli ut comederitis fructum eius et bona illius, Hier. 2
I brought you into the land of Carmel to eat its fruit and its good things, (Jer. 2,7)
Only the honor and glory of God dwells on this mount
glory matters nothing to me
happiness
suffering matters nothing to me
fortitude
joy
charity
peace
piety
Now that I no longer desire them, I have them all without desire
Now that I least desire them, I have them all without desire
The more I desired to possess them, the less I had
The more I desired to seek them, the less I had
and even on the Mount nothing
nothing nothing nothing nothing nothing nothing
goods of heaven
glory joy knowledge consolation rest
goods of earth
possessions joy knowledge consolation rest
neither this
nor this
nor this
nor this
nor this
nor this
neither this
nor this
nor this
nor this
nor this
nor this
To reach satisfaction in all
desire satisfaction in nothing.
To come to the knowledge of all
desire the knowledge of nothing.
To come to possess all
desire the possession of nothing.
To arrive at being all
desire to be nothing.
The way of the imperfect spirit
To come to enjoy what you have not
you must go by a way in which you enjoy not
To come to the knowledge you have not
you must go by a way in which you know not
To come to the possession you have not
you must go by a way in which you possess not.
To come to be what you are not
you must go by a way in which you are not.
The path of Mount Carmel the perfect spirit
When you delay in something
you cease to rush toward the all
To go from the all to the all
you must deny yourself of all in all.
And when you come to the possession of the all
you must possess it without wanting anything.
The way of the imperfect spirit
In this nakedness the spirit
finds its quietude and rest, for in
coveting nothing, nothing tires it
by pulling it up, and nothing oppresses it
by pushing it down, because it is in
the center of its humility.

Here is a simplified version:

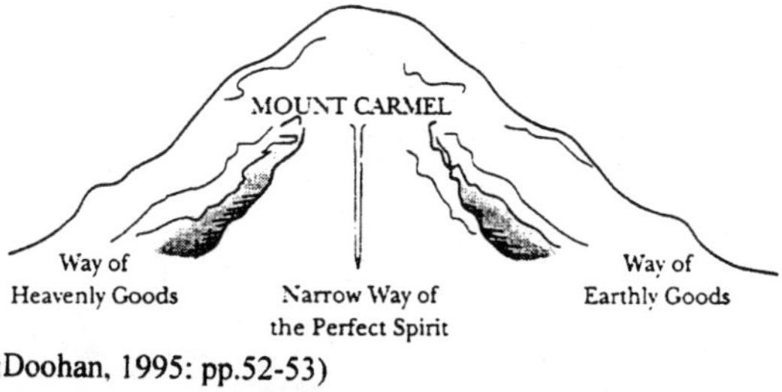

MOUNT CARMEL
Way of Heavenly Goods
Narrow Way of the Perfect Spirit
Way of Earthly Goods

(Doohan, 1995: pp.52-53)

Bibliography

Abbott, SJ, Walter M. (Ed.) (1966). *The Documents of Vatican II*. New York, NY: Guild Press.

à Kempis, Thomas. (N.D.). *The Imitation of Christ*. London & Glasgow: Collins Clear-Type Press.

Alberione, SSP, STD, Rev. James. (1978). *Mystical Union with God through the Nine Degrees of Prayer*. Boston, MA: St. Paul Editions.

Arintero, OP, STM, The Very Rev. John G. (1978). *The Mystical Evolution in the Development and Vitality of the Church*. Vols. 1 & 2. Rockford, IL: Tan Books and Publishers, Inc.

Aumann, O.P., Jordan. (1980). *Spiritual Theology*. London: Sheed and Ward Ltd.

Babinsky, Ellen L.; trans. (1993). *Marguerite Porete: The Mirror of Simple Souls*. Mahwah, NJ: Paulist Press.

Buber, Martin. (1947). *Between Man and Man*. London: Collins Clear-Type Press.

Coussade, SSJ, Fr. J.P. (1959). *Self-Abandonment to Divine Providence*. Rockford, IL: Tan Books and Publishers, Inc.

Crawford, Charles; trans. (1990). *A Mirror for Simple Souls: The Mystical Work of Marguerite Porete*. New York, NY: The Crossroad Publishing Company.

Cunningham, Lawrence S, and Egan, Keith J. (1996). *Christian Spirituality: Themes from the Tradition.* Mahwah, NJ: Paulist Press.

Doohan, Leonard. (1995). *The Contemporary Challenge of John of the Cross: An Introduction to His Life and Teaching.* Washington, DC: Institute of Carmelite Studies Publications.

Dubay, S.M., Thomas. (1989). *Fire Within.* San Francisco, CA: Ignatius Press.

Forman, Robert K.C. (1991). *Meister Eckhart: The Mystic as Theologian.* Rockport, MA: Element, Inc.

Gabriel of St. Mary Magdalen, OCD. (1990). *Union with God According to St. John of the Cross.* Eugene, OR: The Carmel of Maria Regina.

Gallagher, Ph.D., Donald. (1991). "Sum of Perfection," in *IV San Juanista '91, Carmelite Digest,* Vol. 6, No. 4, Autumn 1991.

Garrigou-Lagrange, O.P., Fr. Reginald. *The Three Ages of the Interior Life: Prelude of Eternal Life.* Rockford, IL: Tan Books and Publishers, Inc.
—(1947) Volume One
—(1948) Volume Two

Goichon, Amélie; trans. Bouchard, M.A. (1959). *Contemplative Life in the World.* St. Louis, MO: B. Herder Book Co.

Hollywood, Amy. (1995). *The Soul as Virgin Wife: Mechthild of Magdeburg, Marguerite Porete, and Meister Eckhart. Studies in Spirituality and Theology 1.* Notre Dame, IN: University of Notre Dame Press.

Hughes, Serge & Elizabeth; trans. (1982). *Jacopone da Todi—The Lauds.* Ramsey, NJ: Paulist Press.

Johnston, William. (Ed.) (1973). *The Cloud of the Unknowing and the Book of Privy Counseling.* New York, NY: Doubleday.

Kane, O.C.D., Sr. Aletheia; trans. (1984). *Elizabeth of the Trinity: Major Spiritual Writings—Complete Works,* Vol. I. Washington, DC: Institute of Carmelite Studies Publications.

Kavanaugh, O.C.D., Kieran; and Rodriguez, O.C.D., Otilio, trans. (1979). *The Collected Works of St. John of the Cross.* Washington, DC: Institute of Carmelite Studies.

Kavanaugh, O.C.D., Kieran; and Rodriguez, O.C.D., Otilio, trans. *The Collected Works of St. Teresa of Avila*. Washington, DC: Institute of Carmelite Studies Publications.
—(1976).Vol. 1 *The Book of Her Life*
—(1980).Vol. 2 *The Way of Perfection / The Interior Castle*
—(1985).Vol. 3 *The Book of Her Foundations*

Libreria Editrice Vaticana. (1994). *Catechism of the Catholic Church*. Liguori, MO: Liguori Publications.

McGinn, Bernard. (1998). T*he Flowering of Mysticism: Men and Women in the New Mysticism — 1200-1350, The Presence of God: A History of Western Christian Mysticism*. New York, NY: The Crossroad Publishing Company.

McGinn, Bernard (Ed.). (1994). *Meister Eckhart and the Beguine Mystics: Hadewijch of Brabant, Mechthild of Magdeburg, Marguerite Porete*. New York, NY: The Continuum Publishing Co.

Merton, Thomas. (1977). *The Collected Poems of Thomas Merton*. New York, NY: New Directions.
—(1951). *The Ascent to Truth*. New York, NY: Harcourt Brace and Company.
—(1948). *The Seven Storey Mountain*. New York, NY: Harcourt Brace and Company.

Murk-Jansen, Saskia. (1998). *Brides in the Desert: The Spirituality of the Beguines*. Maryknoll, NY: Orbis Books.

Muto, Susan. (1991). *John of the Cross for Today: The Ascent*. Notre Dame, IN: Ave Maria Press.

Petroff, Elizabeth Alvilda. (1994). *Body and Soul: Essays on Medieval Women and Mysticism*. New York, NY: Oxford University Press.

Poslusney, O. Carm., Rev. Venard. (1973). *Attaining Spiritual Maturity for Contemplation: According to St. John of the Cross*. Hauppauge, NY: Living Flame Press.

Rahner, Karl; trans. Bourke, David. (1971). *Theological Investigations 7*. New York: Herder and Herder.

Roberts, Bernadette. (1993). *The Experience of No-Self: A Contemplative Journey*. Albany, NY: State University of New York Press.

—(1991). *The Path to No-Self: Life at the Center.* Albany, NY: State University of New York Press.

—(1989). *What is Self?: A Study of the Spiritual Journey in Terms of Consciousness.* Austin, TX: Mary Botsford Goens.

St. Teresa. (1930). *The Interior Castle.* London: Thomas Baker.

Zum Brunn, Emilie and Epiney-Burgard, Georgette. (1989). *Women Mystics in Medieval Europe.* New York, NY: Paragon House.

Index

A

B

C

I

J

K

L

M

N

O

P

Q

R

S

T

U